THE DAILY LECTIONARY

A weekly guide for daily Bible reading
The Sundays after Pentecost
Year One, Book Two

Joseph P. Russell

The Daily Lectionary
A weekly guide for daily Bible reading
The Sundays after Pentecost
Year One, Book Two

A method of daily Bible reading that will add to our appreciation of scripture, and to our experience of worship and daily Christian living is provided by the Episcopal Church's The Book of Common Prayer, the Anglican Church of Canada's The Book of Alternative Services and The Lutheran Book of Worship.

In each of these we find a daily lectionary, a listing of passages of scripture for daily reading. The lectionary covers a two year cycle. After following the full cycle, the reader will have been exposed to all of the books of the New Testament twice and all of the pertinent portions of the Old Testament books once—pertinent because the daily lectionary does not include those portions of the Hebrew Scripture that are redundant or irrelevant for the Christian. The Book of Psalms is read in its entirety every seven weeks.

The biblical texts follow the ebb and flow of the liturgical church year. Occasionally they reflect the Sunday texts assigned in the eucharistic lectionary. Since the liturgical seasons take us through the fullness of Christian doctrine, we are exposed week in and week out to all aspects of what it means to be alive in Christ. Of all the many methods of Bible reading, this one is tied most closely to what is going on in the rest of the church.

This pattern of Bible reading goes back to our Jewish roots where portions of scripture were (and still are) assigned for study each week. The entire assembly focused on the same texts. Though the texts were often read in the privacy of one's home, they were still read in communion with the rest of the assembly. This is the principle of the daily lectionary as it exists today in the Christian tradition. Some people will read the lectionary with a group of other worshippers. Others will read the scripture alone. But either way, they will read the Bible with the church. We are in communion with each other.

This weekly guide is designed to be read on Sunday or Monday. Just as you may find help in appreciating a film, concert or sporting event by reading program notes before the event, so you may find help in appreciating your Bible study by reading the program notes offered in this book. Comments provide an overview of the Old Testament, epistle and gospel texts assigned for the week. They include some background on the theological and historical setting along with the rationale for reading the texts during the particular season. Comments also give insight about the rites, hymns, customs of the church, or our calling to act for Christ in the world. *Forward Day by Day* offers notes about the readings. Both resources are offered by Forward Movement to support you in your desire to understand and to be empowered by daily Bible reading.

A few notes for your consideration:

• Forward Movement's *Daily Prayer and Bible Study with the Book of Common Prayer* will help you understand the structure of Morning and Evening Prayer, the context for the Bible texts assigned in the lectionary.

• The daily lectionary readings are shown on pages 936-964 of The Book of Common Prayer; pages 452-475, The Anglican Church of Canada's The Book of Alternative Services; pages 97-99, The Lutheran Book of Worship.

• The daily lectionary follows a sequential pattern of reading scripture each day beginning Monday and running through Saturday. With the exception of the Old Testament, the Sunday readings assigned in the daily lectionary usually have no connection whatsoever with the rest of the week. Therefore, only the readings appointed from the Old Testament for Sundays are considered.

• The psalms are read on a seven-week cycle. The New English Bible with the Apocrypha, Oxford Study Edition (also available in The Revised Standard Version) gives excellent, brief explanations of the psalms. You may want to read the psalms from the annotated Bible rather than from your prayer book on occasion so that you can appreciate the finer points.

•This volume includes notes for the season after Pentecost.

In The Book of Common Prayer and The Book of Alternative Services the weeks are given numbered propers which are keyed to the calendar dates of the Sundays. These proper numbers do not correspond to the numbered Sundays-after-Pentecost shown on church bulletins and liturgical calendars. Look instead at the date assigned for each set of propers shown in the Prayer Book daily lectionary. To make following the daily lectionary easier, the Church Hymnal Corporation has published the texts for the lectionary in four volumes, avoiding the need to look up three different readings in the Bible each day. (*Daily Office Readings*, compiled and edited by Terrence L. Wilson, The Church Hymnal Corporation, 800 Second Avenue, New York, NY 10017)

May scripture come alive for you as you become immersed in the world of the Bible with daily reading. May your life be empowered as you see more clearly the presence and power of God revealed through the pages of scripture. "For whatever was written in former days was written for our instruction, that by steadfastness and by the encouragement of the scriptures we might have hope." (Romans 15:4). We study the Bible not simply for an understanding of the past but for a clearer perception of how God is working in history and in creation today. This is what makes Bible study so exciting and so important for each Christian.

Blessed Lord, who caused all holy Scriptures to be written for our learning: Grant us so to hear them, read, mark, learn and inwardly digest them, that we may embrace and ever hold fast the blessed hope of everlasting life, which you have given us in our Savior Jesus Christ; who lives and reigns with you and the Holy Spirit, one God for ever and ever.

(Book of Common Prayer, page 236)

Joseph P. Russell

Week of the Sunday closest to May 11

The Old Testament readings:

On Monday and Tuesday we read a psalm written by an unknown prophet who lived during the time our biblical ancestors returned from exile in Babylonia, about 500 years before the time of Jesus. Our people returned filled with hope and dreams of a restored nation whose very heart and center would be the Temple in Jerusalem. This hope soon turned to despair as their once beautiful city of Jerusalem continued to lie in ruins. Other people inhabited the homeland of the Jews, people who ridiculed the dreams of a once proud nation. In this historic situation, the psalmist wrote his entreaty to God. He pleaded the people's cause before God. The Lord himself had redeemed the people in the past. Why does he not "come down" now and shake the heart of his people so that alien peoples can know the mighty power of the God of Israel?

Wednesday's and Thursday's readings seem to be an answer to the psalmist's plea. God has seen the people totally reject the covenant. They have broken every commandment to the eating of swine flesh. Surely they have earned God's judgment. Still, despite the evil ways of the people, a remnant shall be saved for a new day with the Lord. The primitive church saw the promise of a restored remnant as applying to the followers of Jesus.

There is hope at the last, the prophet said. God will create "new heavens and a new earth." (Isaiah 65:17a). A perfect reign of justice and peace shall come. Long life will be the gift. Even the lion and the lamb will feed together. The "holy mountain" mentioned in the text is Jerusalem, the sacred city.

Friday's and Saturday's readings continue in a hopeful vein. "Heaven is my throne and the earth is my footstool..." (Isaiah 66:1a). The empty formalism of Temple practice must not replace a "humble and contrite" spirit. (Isaiah 66:2b). Empty rites must not replace the awareness of the downtrodden. It is the humble and the oppressed whom God is concerned about, not the intricacies of the Temple cult. Peace will come like an overflowing river, words that may be familiar from a well-known spiritual based on this text.

The Epistle readings:

We spend this week in the Second Letter of Paul to Timothy, one of the three "pastoral epistles," so called because each deals with the pastoral concerns of the primitive church. Many scholars feel that though these epistles are attributed to Paul, in fact they were written by disciples of Paul at a later date. Other scholars think the pastorals are, indeed, from the hand of Paul himself, written at the time of his imprisonment in Ephesus or Rome. (Second Timothy purports to have been written from Rome.) If second generation disciples of Paul wrote the letters they would have placed the writings within the framework of Paul's life in order to draw on the authority of their teacher. This was common practice at the time. It was simply a means of passing on the authority of a leader or teacher from one generation to the next. Suspicion about Paul's authorship stems from the concerns of the pastoral epistles. Paul lived with the expectation that Christ would return very soon to begin the reign of God. The pastorals seem to have been written at a time when Christians were beginning to realize that they had to be ready for the long haul in the present age, thus the letters deal with church leadership, the authority of scripture, avoiding false teachings, church polity and other such matters of pastoral and administrative concerns.

Read Acts 16:1-5 to learn of Timothy's place in Paul's ministry. And now, a few things to look for as you read the Second Letter to Timothy. Note on Monday the reference to "sound words" and the need to "...guard the truth that has been entrusted to you..." (2 Timothy 1:13-14). Faith, teaching and truth are now equated with a specific doctrine that must be treasured and guarded against the heresies of the time. An ancient hymn may lie embedded in Tuesday's reading: "If we have died with him, we shall also live with him; if we endure we shall also reign with him..." (2 Timothy 2:11-13).

Paul's own struggles were perceived by him as a part of the

suffering that would lead to the victory of Christ's resurrection. Suffering is not empty and meaningless. In Christ it is life-giving as one identifies personally with the suffering of Christ. Notice on Thursday the emphasis on the importance of scripture in equipping the Christian "...for every good work." (2 Timothy 3:17). These words remind us of the role of scripture in our lives. We read so that we may be properly equipped "for every good work."

Paul's warning that the final days will be a time of total decadence and great stress is a concern that Jesus had as he offered his disciples the Lord's Prayer. The petition to "save us from the time of trial" or "lead us not into temptation" refers to this final time of temptation and trial before the second coming.

The Gospel readings:

A week ago we read, "When the days drew near for him to be received up, he set his face to go to Jerusalem." (Luke 9:51). We continue our walk with Jesus this week as he moves deliberately toward his appointment with crucifixion. Along the road he encounters those who would tempt him away from the fulfillment of his saving role in history. The Pharisees and Saducees could not accept his radical interpretation of the covenant. His own disciples and those who drew close to hear his word along the road were not much more receptive. Those who would follow Jesus must know the cost of their discipleship. The time is short.

Decision is the demand of Jesus in Monday's reading. When one is cleansed of "unclean spirits" one must replace allegiance to evil with allegiance to Christ. A passive neutrality will not do. The same point is made to the woman who cries out to Jesus about the blessedness of his mother in giving him birth. "Blessed rather are those who hear the word of God and keep it!" is Jesus' sharp response.

Jesus has been healing and teaching among the people since his baptism by John. His words and actions have been clear indications that the promised judgment and deliverance of God is close, and yet the people stand around asking for signs of

God's presence among them. How could any sign be clearer than what Jesus has been doing among the people, he asks in Monday's reading. The people of Ninevah were quick to repent when the prophet Jonah preached to them. The Queen of Sheba visited King Solomon (1 Kings 10:1-13) to listen to his wisdom. The people of Ninevah and the Queen of Sheba, enemies and aliens of Israel, will stand in judgment over Israel in the days to come, for they at least had sense enough to respond to the preaching and wisdom of God.

Tuesday's reading is a strong condemnation of the Pharisees and lawyers who challenge his words and acts. To appreciate Jesus' denunciation of the religious hierarchy of his day, replace the words "pharisee and lawyers" with "church leaders."

Jesus' words read on Wednesday are a grim foretaste of the Christian persecution to come. Read these words with thoughts of Christian persecutions that continue where the Gospel confronts oppressive leaders. Bishop Desmond Tutu and many other Christians in South Africa find themselves facing imprisonment and even death as they witness to the justice that Christ demands. The Gospel is a radical power that threatens the unjust orders that enslave people in political and economic servitude.

A difficult statement greets us midweek: "And every one who speaks a word against the Son of man will be forgiven; but he who blasphemes against the Holy Spirit will not be forgiven. And when they bring you before the synogogues and the rulers and the authorities, do not be anxious how or what you are to answer or what you are to say; for the Holy Spirit will teach you in that very hour what you are to say." (Luke 12:10-12). The Interpreter's Bible explains that ". . .blasphemy against the Holy Spirit is probably to be understood in the light of verse 12. The unbeliever who speaks against Christ will be forgiven, but not the believer who refuses to confess faith when supernaturally prompted to do so."*

---

*The Interpreter's Bible, Volume 8, p. 224, Abingdon Press).

On Thursday, the emphasis shifts from confrontation and warnings of judgment to instruction on discipleship. The values of the disciple are not to be the values of society, Jesus warns.

The necessity for the disciple to make a radical decision for Christ is again emphasized as we end our week in Luke. Jesus came to force a decision on the believer. There can be no compromise with the proclamation of the Gospel. Acceptance of one's discipleship will inevitably bring conflict even within families. Time was running out. Jesus foresaw his "baptism" that would inaugurate the reign of God. Disciples will find themselves facing the same baptism with Jesus. With these somber words of warning, we end our week in the Gospel.

Week of the Sunday closest to May 18

The Old Testament readings:

The Book of Ruth—a charming story of King David's great-grandmother whose commitment to her mother-in-law, Naomi, serves as a model of devotion for succeeding generations—is our focus through Friday of this week. The story also acted as an introduction to Israel's greatest king. To understand the book, you need a few facts about Old Testament law and traditions.

First, realize that if a man had no male heirs it was like being condemned to extinction. Eternal life was not a part of the understanding of the Israelites. Life was carried on in one's sons.

Secondly, to preserve the male line, brothers and male relatives had the obligation to marry a widow with the hope that a son would be born through the marriage. Property, also, depended upon the male relatives for restoration. Naomi had a small piece of property in Israel, but it would take a male relative to redeem it for her. A quick reading of Leviticus 25:25 and Deuteronomy 25:5-10 will provide you with scriptural reference points for the Book of Ruth.

Thirdly, realize the risk that Ruth took as she decided to go with her mother-in-law to a strange land. She could foresee no rights in Israel, while she might have enjoyed some rights as a woman in her own land. Women were simply considered a man's property. A widow was helpless. Thus, Ruth moved out in faith much as Abraham and Sarah moved out in faith many generations before.

The Book of Ruth may have been written during the reign of David or Solomon as a means of providing added authenticity for David and his line of male heirs on the throne. Some scholars, however, think the book was written after the Babylonian exile during a time when foreign wives were being rejected because they were seen as evil in the sight of God. Ruth provided a strong counterbalance to such exclusive tendencies.

King David's great-grandmother was, after all, a foreigner.

You may recognize familiar words in Monday's reading: ". . .for where you go I will go, and where you lodge I will lodge. . ." (Ruth 1:16). This statement is sometimes read or sung at weddings. Now we see these words in their proper context—words of commitment said by a woman to her mother-in-law. The liturgical greeting, "the Lord be with you," will also be a familiar phrase on Tuesday, a reminder that our liturgical traditions have deep roots.

Ruth gleaned in the fields of Boaz. Another bit of quick research will help you understand that custom. At harvest time some of the crops had to be left in the field for the poor to harvest for themselves. See Deuteronomy 24:19-22 and Leviticus 19:9-10.

In Wednesday's reading, Naomi realizes that Boaz offers the opportunity to exercise the next-of-kin rights. She "primes the pump" a bit with her instructions to Ruth about meeting Boaz on his threshing floor. The actions of Ruth and Boaz that you will read about on Thursday symbolized an offer and acceptance of marriage. Your imagination may lead you to think of more than a symbolic encounter between them. Certainly there is a seductive quality about Ruth's visit, but the purpose of her action was to institute a marriage that would assure the family line of Boaz' next of kin.

Interesting legal customs of ancient Israel become evident for us in Friday's reading. Boaz waits at the town gate for the other eligible relative to come along and for 10 men who could render judgment in the case. The town gate was the courthouse for each community and a quorum of 10 men served as judges in legal cases. The other male relative was interested in the property rights but not the marriage rights, thus leaving the way open for Boaz both to marry Ruth and reclaim the piece of land.

On Saturday we turn to the Book of Deuteronomy. I'll discuss that book in next week's program notes, since we will be studying Deuteronomy for the next two and half weeks.

The Epistle readings:

My remarks of last week concerning the pastoral epistles apply to this week's reading of First Timothy.

The familiar saying, "Christ Jesus came into the world to save sinners," (1 Timothy 1:15) is seen in its biblical context on Monday. Paul, or the disciples of Paul, was obviously quoting a saying in circulation within the church. It could have been a creedal statement or a fragment of a hymn. Tuesday's reading, 1 Timothy 1:18—2:8, includes directives for the gathered church at prayer that still guide us as we share the prayers of the people at the Holy Eucharist. On Wednesday, qualifications for bishops (the Greek word is *episkopos*) and deacons are given in 1 Timothy 3:1-16. Significantly, only two orders of ordained ministers are listed here.

In 1 Timothy 5:19, assigned for Friday, we come across the Greek word, *presbyteros*, translated elder. John Calvin and John Wesley saw this as evidence that elders and bishops were terms used interchangeably in the primitive church. In other words, they claimed that *episkopos*, bishops, and *presbyteros*, elders, were really one order of ordained ministry, rather than two separate orders. They based this claim partly on the scriptural references read this week. It was on this authority that John Wesley ordained two men as *presbyteros* or elders and sent them to the mission field in America. Since Wesley had been ordained in the Church of England as a *presbyteros* and that was used interchangeably with the term, *episkopos*, or bishop, in the New Testament, he reasoned that he had the authority to ordain other *presbyteros*. From such sources come the struggles that still divide the church of Christ today.

Watch for another ancient Christian hymn in 1 Timothy 3:16— "He was manifested in the flesh, vindicated in the spirit..." We can say that the first hymnal of the church was the New Testament itself—enriched by a tradition of hymns and canticles, with texts from the Old Testament as well as the New Testament.

"For the love of money is the root of all evil..." (1 Timothy 6:10). Sound familiar? Well, here is its origin, though the writer of this epistle may have picked up a saying familiar in the ancient world and used it to illustrate his point.

The Gospel readings:

The demand for decision is the theme we launch our week with. Jesus is questioned about the death of people killed as a result of persecution and accident. Was their death a punishment from God? No, he assures them, but let their deaths be a warning of your own need to act now. Life can be snuffed out in an instant. God expects the disciple to bear fruit. Jesus' warning about decisive action for the Gospel is heightened with the parable of fig tree: "And if it bears fruit next year, well and good, but if not, you can cut it down." (Luke 13:9).

The words we read this week must be taken very seriously. Our quest for power and success in the world must not come before our primary task of standing with Christ for justice and healing. That is what it means to bear fruit in the kingdom of God. Pious language or complacent participation in church life cannot be equated with following Christ.

On Friday and Saturday we find ourselves sitting at table with Jesus in the home of a Pharisee. The dinner table conversation provides a metaphor that Jesus used to talk about humility as well as a context for Jesus to tell the parable of the wedding feast. The parable confronts the institutional church of our own day. We, like the Jews of Jesus' time, are invited to be God's witnesses in the world, but it is often the outcasts whom God must bring in to sit at table. We are bound by our possessions and worldly responsibilities, too busy and involved to respond.

Week of the Sunday closest to May 25

The Old Testament readings:

The next two and a half weeks we will be reading from the Book of Deuteronomy. For the historical setting of the book, take a moment and read 2 Kings 22:3—23:3. King Josiah, one of Judah's last kings before the Babylonian exile, began a major religious reform. The Book of Deuteronomy was the cornerstone of that reform. Supposedly discovered in the Temple during its reconstruction, the book purports to be words spoken by Moses just before his death and the entrance of our biblical ancestors into the Promised Land. In fact, the book appears to have been written in King Josiah's time or a few years earlier (640-609 B.C.). Deuteronomy is a part of an extended narrative that provides a summary of Israel's history from the time of Joshua and the taking of Canaan up to the time of Josiah. The Book of Deuteronomy and the historic narrative are written from a distinct viewpoint: when the people of Israel follow the covenant, they prosper from the Lord's blessing; when they break the covenant, they suffer at the hand of God who raises up enemies and natural disasters to chastise a wayward people.

The need to remember the mighty acts of God in order to remain faithful to the covenant is another recurring theme in Deuteronomy. Remembrance of the past leads to consciousness of God's presence in every generation. To forget the mighty acts of the past is to forget the covenant. Psalm 78:1-8 stresses this theme in a succinct way. (Mt. Horeb is the Deuteronomic writer's name for Mt. Sinai.)

Tuesday's reading makes reference to Moses' punishment by God. "Furthermore the Lord was angry with me on your account, and he swore that I should not cross the Jordan . . ." (Deut. 4:21). As background for that statement read Numbers 20:1-12, Deuteronomy 1:19-40 and Deuteronomy 32:48-52. The people's faithless fear of the inhabitants of Canaan and Moses' action in drawing water out of the rock in the wilderness of Zin were perceived as the reasons Moses and the people were forced to wander in the wilderness for a generation. Why the

Lord was perceived as being angry with Moses for striking the rock is not clear from the text, unless there is an inference that Moses was attempting to claim credit for the miracle himself.

The Ten Commandments or Decalogue is Friday's reading. Just before the recitation of the commandments, Moses again rehearsed God's mighty acts for Israel. In response to God's actions for Israel, the people were called into a covenant relationship with the Lord. This writing follows the ancient pattern of covenant-making between a king and a people. The king would rehearse for the people what he had done for them, and he would call them into a covenant relationship. At the Eucharist the priest recalls the mighty acts of God in the prayer of consecration: "Holy and gracious Father: in your infinite love you made us for yourself; and, when we had fallen into sin and become subject to evil and death, you, in your mercy, sent Jesus Christ..." (BCP, p. 362). We then move to the altar for the sacrament, a means of renewing our covenant with God through Christ.

Saturday's reading is a grand scene in which Moses recalls the appearance of the Lord at Mt. Horeb when the covenant was made. The scene may reflect a liturgical celebration in the Temple, enacted periodically to renew the covenant. In the days of the Temple the people would have celebrated the covenant with incense, processions, and great pageantry. We end our week in the Book of Deuteronomy with the beautiful refrain that sets the theological tone of this great work: "You shall be careful to do therefore as the Lord your God has commanded you; you shall not turn aside to the right hand or to the left." (Deut. 5:32).

The Epistle readings:

Paul's Second Letter to the Corinthians will be our focus for the next three weeks. In this letter we see the apostle struggling with issues that were dividing the church in Corinth. We sense his pain, his anger, his love for the people, and most of all his vision of what it means to be given new life in Christ. Conflict is nothing new to the church. With the exception of the Epistle to the Romans, all of Paul's letters were written into situations of conflict and disagreement.

Apparently the church in Corinth had split when several strong persons disagreed with Paul's theological ideas and raised doubts about his authority to preach the Gospel in the first place. A visit from Paul to heal the division ended in disaster. The division in the church only deepened. Paul wrote an angry letter back to the church a short time after he left Corinth. That letter resulted in disciplinary action against the troublemakers and a restoration of unity. What we have in 2 Corinthians is a follow-up letter in which Paul rejoices at the new harmony, but continues to stress his authority and credentials for the future.

The letter opens with a discussion of suffering. Suffering took on meaning for Paul because he saw it as a personal way of participating in the redeeming suffering of Christ. With Paul's words in mind, my aunt offered the pain she suffered from cancer as her living sacrifice to Christ, a way of participating in the healing power of the cross. The reference to Paul's strife in Asia remains a mystery for there is no historic or scriptural record of what happened to him there.

Wednesday's reading reveals the anguish Paul experienced as he related to the Corinthian church. He felt so badly that he had been a part of the pain felt by the people. He could not face another painful visit in Corinth.

Having expressed his feelings, Paul could turn to the more ethereal matters of theology. The glory known in Christ is far beyond the momentary glory experienced by Moses when he received the covenant. (A description that is fresh in our minds from the reading of Deuteronomy this week.) The Torah placed a barrier between God and people. Though Torah pointed out the way of righteousness, no one could walk in that way, for the very covenant that promised righteousness in the Lord also pointed out the hopeless sinfulness that separated one from God. In Christ, the barrier had been removed. One living in union with Christ reflects his glory and is transfigured into the likeness of Christ as the relationship deepens.

Watch for familiar quotations as you follow the lectionary readings on Friday and Saturday: "For what we preach is not ourselves, but Jesus Christ as Lord." (1 Cor. 4:5) ". . .because we look not to the things that are seen but to the things that are unseen; for the things that are seen are transient, but the things that are unseen are eternal." (1 Cor. 4:18).

The Gospel readings:

On Monday we "hit the road" again leaving the dinner table of the Pharisee to continue our journey to Jerusalem with Jesus. We pick up again the familiar theme of the cost of discipleship that we've been dealing with these past two weeks. The bearing of the cross of Christ must come even before family responsibilities and certainly before love of self.

In chapter 15 we shift from the difficult words describing the demands of the Gospel to look at the good news of the grace proclaimed in the Gospel. We hear three parables of God's mercy; the parable of the lost sheep, the parable of the lost coin and the parable of the prodigal son. Note that the younger son in that last parable is not accepted because he deserved forgiveness. He was not even particularly remorseful when he got up from the pigsty. He was hungry! Yet the father was "moved with pity."

The grace of the father grasping his son in a "kiss of peace" is hard for the older brother to accept. I would suspect that most of us identify with the elder brother and not the younger as we hear this familiar parable. How hard it is for us to accept the grace that is offered to us as we walk hesitatingly back up the road. As we pass-the-peace in the context of the Eucharist, let us remember that we are called to be "fathers/mothers" to each other by passing on the grace of God revealed in Christ to those around us.

Thursday's reading includes the parable of the dishonest steward. If a dishonest steward knows how to get ready for the master's inevitable judgment, surely the disciples of Jesus should know how to be prepared!

Week of the Sunday closest to June 1

The Old Testament readings:

"You shall therefore love the Lord your God, and keep his charge, his statutes, his ordinances and his commandments always." These words in Deuteronomy 11:1 greet us as we begin our week, words that express the theme of this great writing. The reason for the love of God is then stated in eloquent terms. This Lord whom you are to love with all your heart, soul and mind has led you out of slavery and into the promise of life. Then follows the remembering of those saving acts, in much the same way we heard them rehearsed last week. To remember the past is to bring forth response in the present and a vision of the future. This is the same kind of "remembering" that we are called to do with Jesus Christ. "Do this in remembrance," we hear each time we celebrate the Eucharist together. It is a remembering that calls forth a response from us, a total self-offering to the God revealed in Christ.

The people will be blessed as they follow the law and severely punished as they forget it. They can choose life or death by the way they respond to the covenant, another common theme of Deuteronomy that we read on Monday. "You shall therefore lay up these words of mine in your heart and in your soul; and you shall bind them as a sign upon your hand, and they shall be as frontlets between your eyes." (Deut. 11:18). These poetic words of commitment were literalized by later Jews. The phylactories, mentioned by Jesus, were pouches worn by Jews at prayer. Part of today's reading, along with three other passages from the Torah, were carried in the pouches as a way of fulfilling this commandment. "And you shall teach them to your children, talking of them when you are sitting in your house, and when you are walking by the way, and when you lie down, and when you rise." (Deut. 11:19). This beautiful statement lies at the heart of our tradition of the daily offices. We begin, live and end with each day framed in God's word and covenant.

One of King Josiah's concerns was to centralize the cultic worship of the people at the Temple in Jerusalem. You will see this concern expressed in Tuesday's reading, a theme that is repeated all through the Book of Deuteronomy.

Our reading in 2 Corinthians adds meaning to Wednesday's Old Testament passage. Don't let people posing as prophets and dreamers come and tempt you to follow other gods, is the warning. Paul's anger at the church, expressed in 2 Corinthians, stemmed from just such compromise with the new covenant of the Gospel. Jesus would pose a stern warning to those who tempted the young-in-faith away from his Word. "...but whoever causes one of these little ones who believe in me to sin, it would be better for him to have a great millstone fastened round his neck and to be drowned in the depth of the sea." (Matt. 18:6).

The deep concern for justice expressed in Deuteronomy shapes biblical ethics for the Christian in today's society. The kings of Israel are to live humble lives; they must not be like the arrogant kings of other lands.

A foretaste of our Eucharistic liturgy is offered in Friday's reading. At the three great pilgrimage festivals of the Temple (Passover, Tabernacles and Pentecost), the faithful Jews were to bring the first fruits of their harvest. In the presence of the priests they were to rehearse the mighty acts of God. This was no impersonal recitation of history, but a personal identification of each Jew with what God had done. "He brought *us*" is the clear message. A past event of God's activity becomes a personal statement of faith for each believer. At the Eucharist we, too, rehearse the mighty acts of God in the past and personalize them. We offer our first fruits, our "...selves, our souls and bodies, to be a reasonable, holy, and living sacrifice unto thee..." (BCP, p. 336).

Saturday's reading moves us in time to the days just before our people crossed into the Promised Land. They now stand poised in the land of Moab ready to cross over, and Moses calls them to renew the covenant made at Mt. Sinai, or Mt. Horeb. Again the acts of God are rehearsed. Though the people have seen these acts over the years, they still cannot perceive them. They are still blind and deaf to the Lord's presence among them.

"...but to this day the Lord has not given you a mind to understand, or eyes to see, or ears to hear." (Deut. 29:4). Jesus' frustrations with the blindness of his disciples echoed Moses' statement made at Moab. The disciples, too, had seen God's mighty acts revealed, but could not understand. We would not attribute lack of faith to the Lord's doing, but in the minds of the biblical writers everything that happened was caused by God, even the stupidity of the people.

A portion of Deuteronomy that is not included in our daily office reading would make a nice conclusion. Deuteronomy 8:1- 3, 6-20 is appointed for reading on Thanksgiving Day. The admonition in that reading, so appropriate for us in the United States today, is that we dare not forget what the Lord has done and think we, ourselves, have won the victories of life.

The Epistle readings:

Our second week in Paul's Second Letter to the Corinthians opens with a beautiful statement of reconciliation in Christ. A new order of life has come in which men and women have been reconciled with God through Christ's self-giving act of redemption. Thus, we can all be one in Christ, reconciled with each other as well as with the Lord. This is the fantastic message entrusted to the church of Christ. This is the Good News of the Gospel. Familiar quotations may jump out at you from this letter. "Therefore, if any one is in Christ, he is a new creation..." (2 Cor. 5:17-19).

You may notice that 2 Corinthians 6:14—7:1 is an optional portion of Tuesday's reading. Some scholars think this brief section is a fragment of one of Paul's earlier letters to the Corinthians and this does not belong in its present position. Does it seem out of context to you?

You may remember that last week I talked about an earlier letter of Paul's in which he had strongly condemned the Corinthian church for accepting the false teachings and decadent practices of some members. He had sent Titus to follow up on that letter and waited for what seemed an endless period of time for Titus' report. Writing from Macedonia, Paul tells his Corinthian friends that Titus did at last join him with the good news that the church was once again united in Paul's teaching and authority. Paul's joy flows out of this very personal letter. Read Acts 16:11—17:15 for a picture of the struggles that Paul was going through in the region of Macedonia.

Your experience in a stewardship drive may come to mind as you read the selections appointed for Thursday through Saturday. Having made his peace with the Corinthians and being assured of their devotion to him, Paul can remind them they have not yet completed the fund-raising drive for the church in Jerusalem where the people were suffering from poverty. Their conflict with Paul had interrupted the drive. Now it is time to complete it. The churches of Macedonia are doing a tremendous job of raising money, Paul gently informs them. Surely they can do even better. "God loves a cheerful giver," Paul says, paraphrasing a saying found in the Book of Proverbs. (2 Cor. 9:7). There is no subtlety in Paul's approach.

The Gospel readings:

Jesus approaches Jerusalem with one eye on the Cross, and the other eye on his disciples. This week we read parables and teachings of Jesus meant to guide the life of the disciples in the difficult days to come. Compassion and service to the poor, the need for perseverance in prayer and faith, and eyes open for the signs of the coming kingdom are essential qualities for Christian life.

Midweek we shift from a loose collection of sayings about discipleship to words about the coming day when the reign of God will finally come. The writer of the Gospel of Luke uses the designation ". . .the days of the son of Man" to designate what some would call the "second coming of Christ." This will be a time of final judgment and salvation, a time when God's will is fully ". . .done on earth as in heaven." Jesus uses vivid imagery to convey his demand for faithfulness and patience on the part of the disciples. The cost of discipleship is high. The cost of rejecting the covenant revealed in Christ is yet higher. That was the word for the church of the first and second century. That is the word for the church today.

Week of the Sunday closest to June 8

The Old Testament readings:

The account of the great covenant-making ceremony at Moab before our people moved into the Promised Land continues to be the focus as we begin our reading this week in Deuteronomy. Keep in mind that Deuteronomy was written during the reign of King Josiah (he died in 609 B.C.). The northern kingdom of Israel had already fallen to the Assyrian empire in 721 B.C. The leaders and powerful people of the kingdom were exiled in Assyria, and Judah lived with the dread of such exile themselves. Parts of Deuteronomy were compiled as late as 550 B.C., after Judah had suffered exile in Babylonia. Thus we are reading back into this early scene what actually happened many years later. The historic struggles and the physical adversities the nation suffered were understood to be the direct result of the people's turning away from the covenant made with God at Mt. Horeb (Mt. Sinai) and again in the kingdom of Moab just before moving into the Promised Land.

Monday's reading offered hope to those exiles who had felt God's judgment in their nation's defeat. God would restore a repentant people—a people who must circumcise their hearts and return to the Lord. That latter phrase may be familiar to you. St. Paul borrowed that rich imagery." (Romans 2:29).

"Today choose life" is the focus for Tuesday's reading. Heaven and earth will be the witnesses to this great covenant-making action between God and the people. Read on to the end of chapter 31 for the conclusion of this vivid scene at Moab. Joshua is to take the spirit of God's leadership from Moses. The succeeding generations must hear and respond to the stories of God's mighty acts in history. They must remember this Covenant. Act and Word must frame their daily response to the Lord, a love of God that is translated into love for neighbor and stranger among them. This, I would add, is the commission of the people of God in every generation. We must pass on the story and the covenant so that the succeeding generations may respond in awe and reverence to the living God who calls them out as their ancestors were called out to witness to the power of God in the world.

Our days in the Book of Deuteronomy end midweek with a prophetic psalm of praise for God's power displayed in Israel's history. The balance of the week is spent in the apocryphal Book of Ecclesiasticus (The Wisdom of Jesus, Son of Sirach).

> Sirach's book is essentially an apology for Judaism. Writing to defend the religious and cultural heritage of Judaism against the challenge of Hellenism, he sought to demonstrate to his fellow Jews in Palestine and the Diaspora, and also to well-meaning pagans, that true wisdom resides in Israel.*

(Diaspora is a technical term meaning the Jews dispersed throughout the world).

The portion of Ecclesiasticus assigned for Thursday through Saturday is a psalm of praise to God for the great leaders of Israel. Moses is one of those heroes, making this reading a fitting tribute to the central figure in the Book of Deuteronomy. The attention given to Moses' brother, Aaron, also reflects the interest in the Temple cult shown by the writers of Deuteronomy, as well as by the writer of Ecclesiasticus.

The Epistle readings:

Prepare for some tough words from Paul this week. He's angry, hurt, defensive of his authority, and threatening a third visit to Corinth to straighten out the recalcitrant church. Many scholars think that the last three chapters of 2 Corinthians are, in fact, the stern letter that Paul referred to several times in our reading over the last two weeks. See if you agree. The theory certainly makes sense. Paul's words of peace and reconciliation shift in these last chapters to angry defense of his apostolic

---

*The Jerome Biblical Commentary. Englewood Cliffs, NJ: Prentice Hall, Inc., 1968; p. 541

authority. The two letters, scholars believe, were simply combined on one scroll with the later letter preceding the first.

Apparently a group within the Corinthian church (or perhaps people coming into the church after Paul left Corinth) has managed to assume authority. Paul sarcastically calls them the "superlative apostles." They preach a different Gospel and ridicule Paul's authority within the church. As you read these chapters, you can hear the adversaries leveling their various charges against Paul by the words of defense he offers. Paul felt the message of the Gospel itself was at stake. The battle went beyond issues of personal leadership, and he defends the Gospel as it had been revealed to him, as well as his authority to proclaim it.

Biting sarcasm is a part of this angry letter. If those superlative apostles are going to boast about their leadership, well let Paul boast. He proceeds to do so in striking terms, revealing his own struggle to proclaim the Gospel in the process. Note that he acknowledges he is not an eloquent speaker. This passage always reminds me of the story in Acts 20:7-12 about the young man who fell asleep during a long sermon and fell out the window.

Part of Paul's boasting leads him to tell of intense visions he had in which he lost all sense of physical feeling. We might well call these "out-of-body" experiences in the sense of feeling "lifted up" into the presence of God. Thursday's reading begins with his description of the experience, though we are not aware that the person described as having a vision was Paul himself until several verses into the assigned text. No one has been able to define the "thorn in the flesh" that plagued Paul and humbled him. The beautiful words in 2 Corinthians 12:9 are often quoted in Christian literature: "My grace is sufficient for you, for my power is made perfect in weakness."

Paul's sarcasm grows more biting in Friday's reading, and we end our week in 2 Corinthians with a threat, or promise, from Paul to return "in power" to speak with apostolic authority. The letter closes with a doxology familiar from Christian liturgy:

"The grace of the Lord Jesus Christ and the love of God and the fellowship of the Holy Spirit be with you all." (2 Cor. 13:14).

The Gospel readings:

Jesus' concern for the poor, the weak and the outcast is expressed in the reading we do this week. Zacchaeus the tax collector is honored as Jesus joins him in his home for a meal. Becoming poor for the sake of the kingdom is held up as an ideal.

The parable of the talents read on Wednesday is sometimes used to justify capitalism and to bless industrious folk who invest their money well, but note the context of this parable. It has nothing to do with investing money and everything to do with using the time between Jesus' departure and his coming again productively for the reign of God. The parable comes right before Jesus' entry into Jerusalem. In a sense, the parable serves as a summary of all the teaching about life after Jesus' resurrection we've been reading about these past few weeks. "I'm leaving you in charge," Jesus might have said, "produce the appropriate fruit of the kingdom".

Notice that the servant who buries his one talent perceives his master as being ". . .a severe man, you take up what you did not lay down, and reap what you did not sow." How often the grace of God is lost as we see instead only a God who stands ready to condemn us.

Week of the Sunday closest to June 15

The Old Testament readings:

This week we move into the Book of 1 Samuel. The books of 1 and 2 Samuel and 1 and 2 Kings offer one continuing narrative we will be reading from now until the middle of October. The history of Israel from the time of the prophet, Samuel, (about 1040 B.C.) through the destruction of the southern kingdom by the Babylonians in 587 B.C. is given in these books. It is not, however, an objective history. It is a theological narrative that often reflects the same theology with which we are familiar from the Book of Deuteronomy. The deuteronomic school continued to write and edit the national history until about 550 B.C., during the time our biblical ancestors were in exile in Babylonia. The writers took the many strands of tradition that had circulated orally for generations and wove those stories together, both editing and adding to the final narrative. Many of those oral stories had already been written on scrolls by the time of the final editing. Each time the nation went through another major change in political structure the important memories of the past that gave shape and meaning to the present were carefully written down for preservation into the next generation. If one final evangelist had taken the four gospels and woven them together, adding his own interpretation to the whole narrative of Jesus, we would have a comparable situation in the New Testament.

The poignant story of Hannah comes to us on Monday. The poor woman prayed so fervently for a child that the priest, Eli, thought she was drunk! If she could just have a child, she promised in prayer, she would give that child to the Lord in total dedication. On Tuesday we learn that the prophet/priest, Samuel, was that child. Notice Hannah's song in 1 Samuel 2 and compare it with Mary's song, the Magnificat, in Luke 1:46-55. Both songs speak of God raising up what is weak and bringing down the mighty. "The bows of the mighty are broken, but the feeble gird on strength." (1 Samuel 2:4). Both songs are attributed to women giving birth to a God-ordained child. The

Revised Standard Version and the New English Bible translate Hannah's word of dedication as lending her son to the Lord (1 Samuel 1:28). The Jerusalem Bible offers a clearer translation of her act: she "made him over" to the Lord.

To understand Wednesday's and Thursday's readings, I need to leap ahead with you to the time of King Solomon. In 1 Kings 2:26-27 we read that the priest, Abiathar, a descendant of Eli, was exiled by Solomon from Jerusalem because he backed Solomon's brother, Adonijah, to become king. The house of Zadok replaced Abiathar, putting an end to a long line of priests coming out of the house of Eli. What we see in this midweek reading from 1 Samuel is an explanation of the downfall of the house of Eli at the time of Solomon. The explanation goes all the way back to Hophni and Phinehas, the unfaithful sons of Eli.

Some confusion surrounds Thursday's reading. Poor old Eli was condemned for not reprimanding his sons, yet we read on Wednesday that Eli had indeed confronted his sons with their sins against God. Here is but one of many examples of how the ancient stories of Israel that circulated independently were often placed side by side in the final edition of Israel's history, even when the stories stood in direct contradiction to each other.

My own Sunday school days as a child return to me as I read Friday's selection that describes God calling Samuel while he sleeps with old Eli in the sanctuary at Shiloh. Three times the Lord calls Samuel, and three times Samuel wakes up the old priest, thinking it is Eli who has called his name. The Lord was calling Samuel to a new destiny.

The Second readings:

This week the Book of Acts of the Apostles becomes our focus. Acts is really Book Two of the Gospel according to Luke. The same author wrote both books, though they are separated in the New Testament by the Gospel according to John. Where the Gospel of Luke relates the Good News of Jesus Christ, the Acts of the apostles proclaims the Good News of the Holy spirit empowering the church to carry on the work of the risen Christ. The book would have been written at about the same time as the Gospel of Luke, from around 75 to 85. It is written for educated Greeks familiar with the historic style of time. The author of Luke/Acts wanted to make clear that the Christian need not wait for the return of Christ at the end of the age to proclaim the reign of God. Christ had empowered the church with the Holy Spirit. In a real sense, Christ had risen within the church and his continuing activity in creation and history would be made known through that church.

After the ascension of Jesus, reported in Acts 1 and in Luke 24:50-51, the gift of the Holy Spirit came to the apostles as they gathered together on the Jewish feast of Pentecost. The feast remembers the giving of the covenant to Moses on Mt. Sinai. It remains a major Jewish festival to this day. Read Exodus 19:14-16 for a description of the thunder and lightning that shook the mountain when Moses prepared to receive the covenant. This imagery is used poetically by the writer of Luke/Acts as he describes the receiving of the Holy Spirit. This moment marks the giving of a new covenant, or testament, to the peoples of the world, one not written on stone, but "written on the hearts of the people," as Jeremiah had said. (Jeremiah 31:33). The tongues spoken by the apostles are not ecstatic tongues of praise, but the tongues of every known language in the world. The convenant made known through he Holy Spirit is one that will be understood and received by all nations and not just by the Jews.

Peter's sermon read on Thursday would not have been recorded word for word at the time it was given. The several sermons ascribed to Peter and Paul in Acts are reconstructions by Luke, based on the proclamation of the Gospel that the church was making at the time. The Hebrew scriptures, especially the book of Psalms, furnished "proof texts" for the Christian evangelists. Thursday's reading contains two quotations from the book of Psalms, words ascribed to King David, though authorship of those psalms is unknown. Jesus is the one who comes to fulfill the words written long ago, Luke wanted to point out.

The Christian evangelists and the writers of the gospels often took their quotations from Hebrew scripture out of context, but they saw in those words entirely new meaning in the light of Jesus' death and resurrection.

The outline of Christian communal life read on Friday must still shape our vision of Christian community today. The people gathered to hear the teaching of the apostles, to share fellowship, to "break bread" (a term denoting the celebration of the Eucharist) and to pray. Out of their common life, shared in the power of the Holy Spirit, came acts of power that amazed the surrounding community. Everything was shared in common so that each person had what they needed. The early Christians were all Jewish so that the Temple was still a major focus in their lives, and yet they would also gather in private homes for the "breaking of the bread."

Saturday's reading repeats the picture of perfect communal life in the primitive Christian church. The Christians fulfilled perfectly the call of the Torah that no one shall be poor. (Deut. 15:4). The story of Ananias and Sapphira, who lied to the apostles and held back the proceeds of the sale of their property, was a story told in the primitive church to emphasize the standards of Christian community.

The Gospel readings:

Our week opens with increasing confrontation between Jesus and the Jewish authorities. It is this confrontation that leads to the cross, but Jesus faces both with grim determination. The parables he tells are parables of judgment against the nation. The parable of the wicked husbandmen we read on Monday, is "aimed at them," the scribes and chief priests realize. They are also "aimed at us" who are appointed in our time to care for the vineyard of God. We must read these words with their historic context in mind, but we cannot leave the words safely in history.

Tuesday's reading is a familar one. Jesus is asked about paying tribute to Caesar with the hope of trapping him. There is irony in Jesus' reply. Everything in heaven and on earth belongs to God. Thus, we render *all* authority to God ultimately. So long as civil authorities do not act against God's will, we may be obedient to them. But God demands an obedience that transcends state, society and even family prerogative.

Thursday's reading about Christ being the Son of David is confusing without a knowledge of the context of the psalm and sonship of King David. The point is that Jesus' role in history and eternity cannot be pinned down to merely being a son of King David. The people expected a descendant of David to become their political messiah and drive out the hated Roman occupation forces.

The psalm Jesus quotes is 110:1: "The Lord says to my lord: Sit at my right hand, till I make your enemies your footstool." The psalm is a promise to Israel's kings that God will defend them until their enemies "become their footstool." The psalms were all attributed to David's authorship in Jesus' day. If the expected messiah is to be the lord of the coming reign of God, and if David wrote the psalm, then the messiah can't be both David's son and David's lord!

Friday's reading speaks of the judgment and trial at the end-time before the reign of God fully comes. Persecution and trial are the roads to salvation, Jesus warns, but through it all, Christians will know in every age that Christ walks with them. It is this intense period of end-time trial that Jesus refers to in the Lord's Prayer with the phrase, "save us from the time of trial and deliver us from evil." (ICET translation of the Lord's Prayer).

The type of writing we read on Friday and Saturday is known as apocalyptic literature, from the Greek word meaning to reveal or uncover. The message of apocalyptic writing is that the people of God will inevitably suffer for witnessing to God's action in the world. The terrible suffering, however, will end in victory for the faithful. The suffering is the trial that leads to fulness in the reign of God. Apocalyptic writing is highly symbolic. It is poetic in its description of the end-times, for only poetry can express this mystery.

The application for us is that we must be alert and ready for

Christ's return at the end-time. There is meaning to our life's struggles. We dare not compromise the call for justice and transformation demanded by the Gospel. To do so is to surrender to the principalities and powers of the present age.

Week of the Sunday closest to June 22

The Old Testament readings:

The priest, Eli, dies at the horrible news of the Ark's capture and the death of his two sons. His daughter-in-law gives birth at the moment the news is conveyed. The child's name of Icabod, meaning "no glory" or "where is the glory?" expressed the anguish of that moment. Names in the Old Testament usually carried a symbolic meaning.

The Philistines were not happy for long, though, about the capture of the Ark. Their god, Dagon, fell down to worship the god of Israel, and, if that was not disheartening enough, a terrible plague broke out in every place the Ark was taken. Realize that the story has been embellished over the years as the event took on added significance. Everything that happened was seen as an act of God. The poor Philistines may have won the physical battle against Israel, but they lost the theological battle! They were only too happy to send the Ark back to whence it came, with appropriate gifts to placate the angry and powerful god of their enemies.

The Ark moved mysteriously, the text implies, to the town of Beth-Shemesh, located near the common border between the Philistines and the Israelites. Finally, the Ark was placed at Kiriath-jearim. We now come to one of the few times of prosperity and peace described in the historic narrative of Israel, and it comes at the time that Samuel—prophet, priest and judge—was dispensing justice throughout the tribal territories of the Israelites. Samuel had now assumed the role of mediator and intercessor once held by Moses and Joshua. He also assumed the priestly role of offering sacrifices, we discover in Wednesday's reading. It is God who wins the great deciding victory over the Philistines, described in chapter 8. The thunder and natural disturbances of nature throw the Philistines into panic. All the Israelites had to do was follow the fleeing Philistines and put them to the sword.

You may notice a major discrepancy between chapter 8, read

on Thursday, and chapter 9, read on Friday and Saturday. Here, again, we see an example of how the final deuteronomic editors placed two entirely different versions of an event side-by- side. The contradictory stories provide us with an interesting commentary on the political and theological struggles that often divided the people.

In Thursday's reading we hear the people demanding that Samuel appoint a king for them. Samuel warns them that to ask for a king is to reject God who is their only legitimate king. The Lord, speaking into the mind of the prophet, authorizes the anointing, but only with deep foreboding. Saturday's reading indicates that the Lord initiates the process of finding a king for his people. The handsome young man Saul is on the way to see Samuel, the Lord informs his faithful prophet, and Samuel is to anoint Saul king. The first account of the anointing of a king for Israel reflects the conservative feelings of one of Israel's political/theological schools. To appoint kings to rule Israel was to become like the other nations who surrounded Israel. The royalist wing of political and theological thought, on the other hand, could see the Lord working in new ways as a nomadic people became a settled nation. It was God who chose the king and ruled the people through him. The anointing with oil expressed that divine commission. Israel was a theocracy in the sense that God ruled the people through the kings.

The word for "anointed" in Hebrew is *messiah*, and in Greek the word is *christos*, or Christ. The Lord's anointed spoke and acted with the authority of God. It is important to realize that as Christians we are also anointed at our baptism ". . .and marked as Christ's own for ever." (BCP, p. 308). Each Christian is a *messiah*, or *christos*, in the sense of being anointed to speak and act for the Lord. In two weeks you will read Acts 10:38 in which Peter points out that Jesus was ". . .anointed. . . with the Holy Spirit and with power. . ." This is the power to which our anointing at baptism points. We are sent forth in power to carry out the work of the Lord in the world today.

The Second readings:

The center of Christian activity remained in Jerusalem, we learn this week as we read from the book of Acts, and opposition to the followers of Jesus was heightened as the power of the Holy Spirit was seen more strongly in the lives of the apostles. Part of Luke's intention in these chapters is to show the increasing opposition of the Jews. Another concern of Luke was to point out how impossible it was to stop the activity of the Holy Spirit in the church. Even prison could not hold back the apostles from proclaiming the Gospel in word and act.

In chapter 6 we are introduced to the Greek-speaking deacons, specifically to St. Stephen, the first Christian martyr. Notice the custom of the laying on of hands to pass on the authority and power of the Holy Spirit. We also see in this account the origin of the order of deacons in the church.

The Gospel readings:

We live in the world, as Jesus said, but we are not of this world. Our ethical standards for the individual and society must be higher than the ethical demands of the world at large, because our lives are meant to point to the coming of God's reign. No wonder Jesus warned of trial and controversy in this life. Herbert O'Driscoll calls the ethics of the coming reign of God "anticipatory ethics." The ethics anticipate the new reign and yet we must be guided by them even in the present age.

We move into more familiar territory, beginning on Tuesday, as we start reading about the preparations for the Last Supper. Our week in the gospel ends with the scene at the Mount of Olives where Jesus prays for strength as the disciples sleep.

Week of the Sunday closest to June 29

The Old Testament readings:

The account of Saul's anointing continues as we begin a new week together in 1 Samuel. Remember from Saturday's reading that Saul was incredulous that the Lord should have chosen him. He was from the least of the tribes of Israel and his family was the least important family in that tribe. Samuel offered Saul three distinct signs that what had happened between them had indeed been confirmed by God. The last of the signs was that Saul would join in the ecstatic actions of a roving band of prophets. The prophets of Samuel's day did not play the same role as the prophets of a later day. The actions of the prophets described in Sunday's passage was inherited by Israel from surrounding cultures. Groups of men wandered the countryside, speaking and dancing in ecstatic trance. It's no surprise that people wondered about a proper young man like Saul adopting the characteristics of those roving bands of men.

On Monday we read a completely different rendition of the appointing of Saul. Finally heeding the demands of the people, Samuel gathered the tribes together at Mizpah and went from family to family within each tribe looking for the proper man by casting of lots which indicated a "yes" or "no" from God. This lot finally fell on the young Saul, who was hiding among the baggage! This account was told by the anti-royalist group in ancient Israel who opposed the idea of a king for the nation.

Back to the royalist school on Tuesday, we find Saul saving the inhabitants of Jabesh-gilead from disgrace by a roving, marauding band of Ammonites. Saul acts with the spirit of God and is immediately accepted and confirmed as king of Israel. Samuel had initiated the act of king-making and now the people confirm it in a joyful investiture. The anti-royalist school provides us with the next scene on Wednesday with Samuel's farewell address to the people. With biting sarcasm he asks why he and his family have been rejected and a king demanded instead. Samuel provides a sign for the people that the Lord does not approve of their demand for a king. Thunder and rain come in a season when rain is not expected.

Always realize that you are reading history through the eyes of those who are making theological statements about people, events and natural phenomena. Nothing happens accidentally in these accounts. Everything is seen as a direct act of God. The important point for us who read these great stories today is to understand how events shaped our people's understanding of God's presence in their lives. We, too, must reflect on our lives and make our statements of faith based on life experiences and perceptions.

In one simple act of offering sacrifice, poor Saul loses favor with Samuel and, therefore, with God, we learn in Thursday's reading. Saul sees his army melting away. Samuel does not appear to offer the necessary preparatory sacrifices for battle and so, to protect the strength of his army, Saul makes the sacrifice instead. From this moment on we see Saul's place in God's favor begin to slip tragically.

Saul's son, Jonathan, is introduced to us for the first time on Friday. We'll meet him again in the coming weeks as he becomes close friends with David. Jonathan's brave, but rash, action against a Philistine outpost turns the tide of battle for the Israelites. Things happen so quickly, we read on Saturday, that Saul does not even have time to consult the Urim and Thummim that are carried by the priest in the ephod.

The Second readings:

Our reading of the Book of the Acts of the Apostles continues with the conclusion of the story of St. Stephen. His martyrdom introduces a new person to the scene. "And Saul was consenting to his death," we read at the end of Monday's assigned reading, a dramatic way of introducing St. Paul.

Watch for another dramatic turn in the narrative with Tuesday's reading. Persecutions in Jerusalem forced the Christians there out into the surrounding country. As a direct result of the persecution, the Christian movement was spread further! The very measures used against the church lead to its growth.

We met Philip last week. He was one of the seven deacons set aside to minister to the widows. Now his healing and preaching ministry begins to lead some of the Samaritan people to conversion. Peter and John confirm Philip's ministry by laying hands on his converts, at which time they receive the Holy Spirit. A sense of apostolic authority is contained in Wednesday's reading, along with the reminder of the power of the Holy Spirit revealed in the life of the church. Eunuchs and Samaritans were considered outcasts by the Jews. Thus the conversion of both the eunuch and the Samaritans is a radical statement of acceptance.

The week's reading of Acts is rounded off with the dramatic story of Saul's conversion on the road to Damascus.

The Gospel readings:

We step into the feelings of Holy Week as we read from the Gospel of Luke this week. The narrative opens with Jesus' arrest and Peter's denial. It is Peter's accent that helps give him away.

The elders, or Sanhedrin, meet with Jesus to prepare their case against him before the judgment seat of Pontius Pilate. Any words he said would be used against him, and they would not be above taking what he said out of context. Jesus knows this and states wearily, "If I tell you, you will not believe; and if I ask you, you will not answer." (Luke 22:67- 68). The title, Son of Man, that Jesus applies to himself was taken from the Book of Daniel (Daniel 7:13) and refers to a heavenly figure who would come out of the clouds to announce the reign of God and the destruction of evil. The Son of Man must suffer as a part of this redeeming action in creation, Jesus states before the Sanhedrin. The term, Son of God, is the one thrown back at Jesus, however. This term was associated with the kings of Israel and Judah. The Lord promised King David that he would ". . . build a house for my name, and I will establish the throne of his kingdom forever. I will be his father and he shall be my son." (2 Samuel 7:13- 14a). The royal sons of David, in other words, would be sons of God; thus the title had political implications. Son of God meant a direct threat to Roman dominance, such as the Zealots were plotting to carry out. The elders have prepared their frame-up and are now ready to lead

Jesus before the Roman governor.

The elders open the case before Pilate with an immediate listing of all the accusations they've managed to come up with, but they meet a resistant Pilate who has a sense for justice even though he lacks the courage to carry it out. Sending Jesus off to Herod is but one more attempt to escape the terrible stroke of decision, but Herod only sends him back with more derision for the prisoner.

The role of women in the Gospel of Luke is striking. Along with Simon of Cyrene who carries the cross of Christ, it is the women who enter most deeply into the suffering of Jesus.

The obscure saying in Luke 23:31, "For if they do this when the wood is green, what will happen when it is dry?" was a proverb of the day meaning if things are bad now, just wait and see what happens next!

Jesus on the cross is in command. He forgives a prisoner as a king would forgive a penitent criminal. The promise to the thief is that ". . .today you will be with me in paradise." (Luke 23:43).

Week of the Sunday closest to July 6

The Old Testament readings:

Jonathan's breaking of the fast that he so disdained in our reading on Saturday comes to light in Sunday's reading. An interesting picture is given of how the Urim and Thummim were used, though the scene may have been reconstructed by a later historian. The priest called for a consultation "with God" which meant casting the Urim and Thummim as one would cast dice. The outcome would indicate a positive or negative answer from God. Obviously the Urim and Thummim were capable of coming up with a "this does not compute" response as well, for Saul despairs when he can not receive an answer. His immediate conclusion is that someone in the group has sinned. Jonathan's bravery overrules Saul's resolve to kill his own son for breaking the fast. Perhaps an animal was offered to appease the Lord.

We've already had one explanation for the Lord's displeasure with Saul. He had taken matters in his own hands to offer sacrifice in Samuel's absence. Now we are given a second reason for his rejection, and the reason is hard for us to accept in the light of compassion and justice. Samuel reports to Saul that the Amalekites must be destroyed. The Lord would place them under the ban, which meant the complete destruction of every person as well as their animals and other property. To break the ban by sparing anything of the enemy was to commit a serious sin against the Lord.

This may sound brutal to us as we look back at those times, and yet these feelings are not so far from our minds as we may think. In time of war, we may conceive that God is on our side; the enemy we fight is evil and must be destroyed. Certainly the dropping of the atomic bomb on the Japanese at the end of World War II was a modern equivalent of the ban. Sermons preached from many pulpits in World Wars I and II, in both this nation and in Germany certainly sounded the trumpet for the Lord's triumphant troops facing the enemies of the Gospel, as the Gospel was perceived.

"We need to realize that the Bible is the oral and written reflections of a community; it is a record of how they perceived God acting in their history . . .the Bible traces a slowly evolving understanding of how God acts in his world. Our people only gradually came to understand that God acts not through armed might but through weakness, vulnerability, and love."* That understanding evolves not only in the biblical record, but in our own personal understanding as well.

In any case, Saul fails to apply the ban, and Samuel announces the complete rejection of the Lord as a result. This rejection does not come without personal pain for Samuel, who still cares deeply for Saul.

The process of finding and anointing the next king of the Israelites must now begin, and the faithful Samuel is directed to the house of Jesse where the Lord points out the young boy, David, as the one who is to be anointed. Our biblical storytellers liked the sense of the least being called to the highest position.

Thursday's through Saturday's readings provide us with two interwoven traditions of how David became a servant and soldier for King Saul. One tradition offers the story of David coming into Saul's court as a "music therapist" to quiet the king down during his severe depressions. The other tradition gives a contradictory account: that David just happens to be on the battlefield bringing supplies to his brothers when the great Philistine fighter, Goliath, makes his challenge to the Israelite troops.

The Second readings:

Our study of Acts continues this week, and it reads like a serialized adventure story. Saul's sudden conversion is met at first by suspicion and then by increased excitement in the church. The hostility of the Jews drives Paul out of the city to Tarsus, his home, and our attention turns once more to the

---

*Joseph P. Russell, *Sharing Our Biblical Story* (Minneapolis, MN: Winston Press, 1979), pp. 7-8.

apostle Peter who is sent by a vision to gentile peoples for the first time. The power of the Gospel penetrates prison doors, overcomes persecution and bridges seemingly impossible gulfs of long-standing prejudice and rejection.

The Gospel readings:

Jesus' death and resurrection is the focus of our last week in the Gospel of Luke. Remember that women play a major role in Luke's Gospel. It is women who become the first evangelists as they announce the Good News of the risen Christ. Joanna and Mary of Magdala are two of the women who accompanied Jesus, along with the 12 disciples. (Luke 8:1-3). From Luke's perspective women as well as men were disciples of Jesus. It was women who had the courage to be with the Lord as he died, and it was women who first proclaimed his resurrection.

Jesus appears again to two disciples as they walk to Emmaus. The story has Eucharistic overtones. We come to the sacrament questioning, doubting, hurting, hoping. The Word of God is offered and interpreted, and then we come to know the risen Christ in the breaking of the bread. The beautiful prayer appointed for Evening Prayer in the Book of Common Prayer expresses the ongoing significance of this story for the church: "Lord Jesus, stay with us, for evening is at hand and the day is past; be our companion in the way, kindle our hearts, and awaken hope, that we many know you as you are revealed in Scripture and the breaking of bread. Grant this for the sake of your love." (BCP, p. 124).

Thursday is our last day in the Gospel according to Luke. We leave the evangelist with the commission of Jesus in our minds: "You are the witnesses of these things. And behold I send the promise of my Father upon you, but stay in the city, until you are clothed with power from on high." (Luke 24:48-49). Those words are addressed to the church of Christ today as much as to the disciples of yesterday.

We begin our reading of Mark on Friday. It will take us through the first week of September. This gospel may have been written for the church in Rome, but that remains conjecture. The Temple in Jerusalem had just been leveled by Roman armies as they crushed the last attempts of Jewish Zealots to overthrow foreign rule. Moreover, the church was undergoing persecution. Christians were being dispersed as conditions in Jerusalem grew worse.

In this painful historic situation, the writer of the Gospel of Mark collected the stories of Jesus that he knew and wove them into a proclamation of Good News. The basic message: Have hope, for the agony of the present time is the dawning of the age of fulfillment that is coming soon! The suffering of Christ is God's way of achieving victory over evil. The battle has been won and Christ, not the evil powers of the present age, is the victor. Those who keep faith in this good news will share both in the suffering and the glory of the risen Christ. That is the core of Mark's gospel.

Mark loses no time getting into the message of the gospel. No birth story precedes the ministry of the Lord. John appears in the wilderness as a rustic Elijah figure to announce the new age, and Jesus comes up out of the waters of his baptism to be led into the wilderness where he, unlike his ancestors in the Sinai wilderness, overcomes the temptations of evil.

The authority of Jesus to drive out evil, to teach, and to call disciples is expressed with power in our reading for Saturday. His presence is living witness that the reign of God has dawned.

Week of the Sunday closest to July 13

The Old Testament readings:

The assigned text from 1 and 2 Samuel and 1 and 2 Kings that we read during the summer months is an adventure story of intrigue, tension and high drama. However, we're going to have to keep our eye on several different schools of historians as we do our reading. Some of the details of the stories will be contradictory.

Our first example comes on Sunday. David seems to be introduced to Saul for the first time, which contradicts his introduction into Saul's court in 1 Samuel 16:14-23, read last Thursday. To quote from Robert Alter,

> Logically, of course, Saul would have had to meet David for the first time either as music therapist in his court or as giant-killer on the battlefield, but he could not have done both. Both stories are necessary, however, for the writer's binocular vision of David. In this case, the influence of a deliberate decision to use two versions seems especially compelling. . . he chose to combine two versions of David's debut, one theological in cast and the other folkloric. . . both were necessary to his conception of David's character and historic role.*

David quickly turns from being hero in Saul's eyes to being a threatening competitor to the throne. The women taunt Saul and praise David with a victory song, which adds to the king's anguish. Since success was always equated with God's favor and failure with God's displeasure, events were perceived with a sacred significance that would add to Saul's jealousy.

Contradictions in the narrative become more marked as the week goes on. On Tuesday we read that Jonathan is able to talk his beleaguered father out of his intent to kill David. Then

---

*Robert Alter, *The Art of Biblical Narrative*, p. 148.

we jump to a strange story of Michal's attempt to save David's life. Wednesday's reading contradicts Tuesday's text, for on this midweek day we read that Jonathan apparently has no knowledge whatsoever of his father's evil intentions toward David. Finally, Jonathan and David make elaborate plans for testing Saul's intentions. Jonathan will shoot arrows into the field to signal secretly to David whether or not his life is in danger. These are quaint details that hold the attention of the listener, but they make little sense when we realize that David and Jonathan have face to face encounters before and after the arrows are shot, making the need for elaborate signals questionable.

David's life as an outlaw comes as he is driven out of Saul's presence by the constant threat of death. David stops at Nob, a sanctuary presided over by the priest, Ahimelech and his family. The showbread, or holy bread, that you will read about on Friday was an interesting custom carried out at sacred sanctuaries of Israel. Twelve loaves of bread (representing the 12 tribes of Israel, perhaps) were placed in the sanctuary and kept there from Sabbath to Sabbath. At the end of the week, 12 fresh loaves were placed in the sanctuary and the priests ate the old ones. This practice could have stemmed from pagan temples where the placing of bread would have been seen as a symbolic feeding of the local diety. For Israel, the bread became a continual thank offering. Bread played a deeply symbolic role in the life of our biblical ancestors for many generations before Jesus "took bread" at the Last Supper.

We end our week with David as he begins to gather family and followers into a disciplined band of roving outlaws. Saul, meanwhile, appeals to his fellow tribesmen: "Don't trust David," he warns them, "he'll never do anything for someone from my tribe of Benjamin."

The Second readings:

Our adventure story from the book of Acts continues this week, giving us a running account of the inevitable spread of the church in the Mediterranean world. More gentile Greeks were converted at Antioch, and we learn that it was in this church that the followers of Christ were first called Christians. The scene shifts once more to Peter and his second miraculous escape from prison. Notice how often imprisonment figures in the lives of the apostles. To be a Christian is to face the power structures of the age in which we live. These stories should remind us to look in the prisons of our own time. We, too, may be persecuting the Word of God as it is enfleshed in the social issues of the 20th century.

On Thursday, we begin a new part of the adventures of Paul. Barnabas and Saul (Paul) are set aside by the laying on of hands for a new work and sent on the first of the three missionary journeys. You will need a map of the missionary journeys of Paul as you read Acts from now until the middle of October. Paul's epistles will take on a new interest for you if you can locate the actual cities in which he spent time. As you read about the church he established, turn to the letters (epistles) he wrote to those churches.

The Gospel readings:

The Jewish people at the time of Jesus waited with anticipation for the ushering in of the messianic age. Evil would be defeated and the Lord's kingdom would triumph. They remembered their nation's history and the grand days of David and Solomon. They dreamed of a new David and a new kingdom. In the prophetic poetry found in the Book of Daniel a figure is introduced in Daniel 7:13 who seems to usher in this day of God's new age: "I saw in the night visions, and behold, with the clouds of heaven there came one like a son of man, and he came to the Ancient of Days and was presented to him..." One of Mark's purposes in writing his gospel was to point out over and over again that this triumphant Son of Man who was expected at the coming of the new age was, in fact, Jesus of Nazareth.

As Mark wrote his gospel, he drew together all the stories he knew that proved Jesus was the expected Messiah. Since it was so obvious that Jesus was the Messiah, the people of the church wondered why so many had not accepted him. This question bothered the writer of the Gospel of Mark, too, and he could only conclude that it was God's intent that the nature of Jesus' role as Messiah should be a secret from many and a revealed truth to few. As you read the Gospel of Mark, watch for the signs of Jesus' authority, as well as for the theme of secrecy about his role as Messiah.

Satan was the master of the present age of darkness. Evil, sickness and death were all the dominion of the kingdom of Satan. People who were mentally or physically ill were thought to be possessed by demons. They lived under the cloud of darkness. Jesus' healings and exorcisms were signs that the victory of God's kingdom of light over the kingdom of darkness had begun.

Only God could forgive sins. Temple priests could accept offerings for the forgiveness of sins, but even they could not pronounce the restoration between man and God. Jesus speaks as God when he states forgiveness and healing to a paralytic lowered to him through the roof of a home. Such a statement would be blasphemy to a Jew. We cannot blame the scribes and Pharisees for their shocked response. Jesus spoke words reserved for God.

Because Jesus acts with the authority of Messiah, he can change the laws of Torah (the first five books of the Old Testament). This is a new age that cannot be contained within the old, he pronounces. "No one sews a piece of unshrunk cloth on an old garment...no one puts new wine into old wineskins..." (Mark 2:21-22).

A Surprising statement is read on Saturday: "...but whoever blasphemes against the Holy Spirit never has forgiveness, but is guilty of eternal sin." (Mark 3:29). Though we cannot know exactly what Jesus had in mind when he made this statement, it is evident that one cannot be healed and forgiven by the Spirit if one denies the power of the Spirit.

Week of the Sunday closest to July 20

The Old Testament readings:

We continue our chapter-by-chapter reading of 1 Samuel this week. Remember that David is an outlaw in the mind of King Saul and his followers. Saul, in the meantime, feels the anguish of the loss of God's favor, as well as the loss of allegiance on the part of a growing number of his people and fighting men. Even his own son, he realizes, is partial to David. Jealousy, increasing anxiety and a growing awareness of doom close in on Saul each day. Our Old Testament readings these weeks are adventure stories of faith shared by our biblical ancestors around the campfires and the family table, as well as in formal storytelling and worship. The story is one of the faltering faith of Saul met by cunning acts of daring on the part of David. The forerunner of Robin Hood, the drama of the early American cowboy, and the excitement of an adventure novel are found in these chapters.

Note in Sunday's reading the manner in which David discerns the will of God. Again, the Urim and Thummin, carried by the priest, are used to get a "yes" or "no" answer from God to a specific question. This primitive method of discerning God's will was replaced in later times by listening to the words of a prophet or king.

David's absolute faithfulness to God's anointed is apparent in Monday's reading. David, hidden in a cave from Saul's constant search for him, has the king at his mercy. The moment of power passes as David refuses to kill the king, who is urinating in the cave within reach of David's sword. Surely Saul will call off his search now, we think, but Saul's mental illness and jealousy quickly shade his memory of David's faithfulness once the day of encounter ends.

David is not above running what we would call today a protection racket. He demands money from the rich man, Nabal, in return for not molesting the man's shepherds, we read on Tuesday and Wednesday. These are lusty tales we read these weeks. David may be the Lord's man headed for kingship, but he lives the life of an adventurer, nevertheless.

A major segment of the outlaw adventures of David is left out of our lectionary reading this week. Part of the unassigned reading in 1 Samuel falls between Wednesday's and Thursday's readings. David seeks the protection of a Philistine prince, promising military assistance to Achish, son of King Moach of Gath, in return for protection and the right to live with his 600 men in Achish's territory. Unknown to Achish, David raids tribes friendly to the Philistines, while indicating to Achish that he has raided towns in Judah. This "double agent" status serves Daivd's purposes well for over a year. He wins favor with his own people in Judah for raiding their enemy's camps. He convinces Achish that he is killing the people of Judah and shares the spoils with his protector. The horrible brutality of David's raids are a part of the accepted pattern of the day.

We read two accounts of Saul's death Friday and Saturday, which may confuse you. On Friday we read that Saul killed himself. Saturday's passage indicates that he was killed by an Amalekite, who may have hoped for a reward in bringing the news to David. Instead he is killed for taking the life of the Lord's anointed. To destroy the Lord's chosen king was to sin against God, a crime punishable by instant death.

The Second readings:

The readings for Monday through Wednesday continue the account of Paul's and Barnabas' first missionary journey. Increasing hostility of the Jews becomes a greater and greater problem. The pattern is set on this first journey. Paul arrives in each town and goes first to the synagogue in an attempt to relate to the Jewish people. Sometimes he is welcomed and even asked to talk to the synagogue community. The more he talks, however, the more radical his words are perceived. Acceptance turns to rejection, and Paul turns from Jew to gentile, going out into the larger community. As the gentiles are converted, Paul carefully trains elders among them to carry on the teaching and work of the church. When Paul leaves, the church carries on with the leadership he has prepared.

Beginning on Thursday, we read about the controversy over Paul's and Barnabas' work in the early church. It is the understanding of the Jews who have converted to Christianity that one must be fully a Jew to become a follower of Christ. "Not so," says Paul and others. There is no need to follow the letter of the Mosaic Covenant to become a Christian.

The first council of the church is called at Jerusalem where Paul and Barnabas give an accounting of their activities among the gentiles and receive the apostles' directive through James, the brother of Jesus. If you read Galatians 1:11-19 you will see that Paul's memory of his trip to Jerusalem is very different from what is described in Acts. In Galatians Paul expresses the direct authority he received from the risen Christ. The writer of Luke/Acts, on the other hand, stresses the unity of the church expressed through the authority of the original apostles acting in council to make decisions for the rapidly growing church.

The Gospel readings:

In last week's gospel readings we heard of the calling of Jesus' disciples and his healing ministry. This week we turn to a section in which the disciples are instructed in parables for their mission in the world, and they receive their first test of will and faith while in a boat on the tossing lake.

The scene opens with Jesus teaching a crowd of people by the lake side. He must step into a boat in order to move far enough out from the people to be seen and heard by them. His voice would carry naturally over the waters. Jesus' teachings meant, "Have faith, my disciples. The seed of the kingdom is sown even now as I talk with you. The harvest will come in God's good time. Proclaim that harvest to all who will hear." The writer of this gospel took the first of the parables and turned it into an allegory that explains why the Gospel is not spreading faster than it is.

Why were not more people convinced that Jesus was the Messiah when his miracles and powerful acts of new life were so obvious? Part of the explanation, Mark believed, lay in the hidden nature of Jesus' words and acts, we learn in Mark 4:9-12.

It was God's will that the Word would remain a treasure for the few and a mystery to the many. The other gospel writers did not share this view.

Wednesday's reading describes the calming of the sea. This brief account is very symbolic. The roaring and heaving seas were calmed and separated by God at creation. The power of God to separate the land from the sea was a sign of his creative power in the face of chaos. Psalm 74:12-14 describes that great act of creation poetically. Psalm 65:7 speaks of the power of God to act upon the storm at sea to bring calm to creation and humanity. Jesus is the embodiment of God's power. He comes to bring calm out of chaos and fear, and a new creation happens in his presence.

The strange story of the Gerasene demoniac is given on Thursday. This story needs to be read with the poet's eye as well as with the historian's interest. Jesus comes to drive out the chaos and disorder in the man's life, just as he stilled the chaos of the water. He can do with demons what he wills. He has power over chaos, evil and darkness. He can create sanity out of madness. The death of the pigs may be shocking to the modern reader, but the story would have provided humor to a people who considered swine unclean.

After words and acts of instruction, Jesus sends his disciples out to proclaim the coming kingdom. They've witnessed the power in their own lives. They've been instructed through parable and vivid experience in the meaning of the kingdom. Now it is their turn to act in Jesus' name.

Week of the Sunday closest to July 27

The Old Testament readings:

The adventures of David continue to be our focus this week, and they are truly adventure stories showing the struggle of David to achieve absolute political power over both the northern tribes of Israel and the southern tribes of Judah.

To see the world through the eyes of Christ, we must have a grasp of how Jesus himself understood life. Jesus was a Jew who lived in the midst of his people's story. As we read the accounts of David, we read the accounts of Jesus' forefather. To understand our Lord, to understand our life in the Lord, we need to step into the historical perspective of his people, who become our people through adoption. Out of the struggles of our biblical ancestors came an understanding of how God works in history and in creation.

And now, to the week's drama. On Sunday we read David's beautiful poem of lament to the dead Saul. The Book of Jashar mentioned in the reading may have been a collection of epic national poems similar to David's dirge. The collection has been lost, but several references are made to the book, giving scholars an idea about its contents.

On Monday we read that David has set up his capital at Hebron, a city south of Jerusalem. Since David was from the tribe of Judah (his family came from the town of Bethlehem) he was able to build a base of power and political authority in that southern tribe. Gaining a political foothold among the northern tribes was not so easy, however. Saul came from the city of Gibeah in the tribal area of Benjamin. Saul's army commander quickly moves to make Saul's son, Ishbosheth, king of the northern tribes. Thus, Saul's kingdom is temporarily split among those in the north still faithful to his memory and authority and the tribe of Judah to the south now living under the authority of their new king, David. When you read what appears to be direct conversations between David and God in this week's text, realize that David is probably casting the Urim and Thummim to receive God's answers to specific questions he asks.

The plot thickens as we read Tuesday's assigned lesson. King Ishbosheth accuses Abner of taking one of Saul's concubines into his own home. This act, if true, would have had more than a sexual motivation. To take Saul's concubine was to claim political power for himself. As a result of that accusation, Abner gives his allegiance to David.

David is anxious to have Saul's daughter, Michal, back in his court because she represents political power for him. Saul was his father-in-law. Therefore, David has claim on Saul's rule. The painful reality of the woman's role in society is made evident as we see Michal's new husband running after her as she is taken to David's court.

Joab, David's chief military officer, murders Abner. David quickly separates himself from Joab's act by going into public mourning. He needs the allegiance of Saul's people. The murder could easily alienate them. Note that Joab receives no punishment for his act.

One murder leads to another, we learn on Thursday. Next it is King Ishbosheth who is killed by his own men who hope to win favor with the powerful king of Judah. We know from our reading what they don't know—King David does not take lightly the murder of another king.

On Friday we read of David's triumph. At last he is proclaimed king over the northern tribes as well as over the southern tribes. What a time of celebration! David quickly moves to solidify his gains. He needs a capital city that will speak of his status and authority over all the peoples of Israel and Judah. The ancient walled city of Jerusalem would provide such a symbol for David. As the city of Washington D.C., lies in no state, so Jerusalem lay in neither northern or southern tribal territories. Walls and fortifications defended it. If David could conquer that stronghold, the victory in itself would be a sign of his power.

The Jebusites who control the city are so confident of their defences that they repeat a sarcastic expression that comes to David's attention—the blind and the lame alone can keep out invading armies. The reference to David's hate of the blind and lame is simply his sarcastic answer to the taunts of the defenders. Verse 8 of chapter 5 has been lost in generations of transmission; translators are not sure of the original meaning of the verse. Words seem to be missing from the original. The reference to the water conduit may have been to a plan for some of David's army to enter the city through its water supply conduit. Note the reference to David being the shepherd to the people in verse 3. This metaphor of leadership was often used in connection with Judah's kings and was, of course, applied to Jesus.

Our week in David's court ends on Saturday with his attempt to bring the Ark of the Covenant into Jerusalem. The Ark was a large decorated box supported by poles by which the Israelites carried the Ark in their wilderness wanderings. It may have contained the stone tablets of the Torah. Since its capture and return by the Philistines some years earlier, it had been kept at Kiriath-jearim, west of Jerusalem. The fact that poor Uzzah dies after touching the Ark is probably coincidence, or it could be caused by his fear and awe of the Ark.

The Second readings:

This week in our reading of Acts we find Paul embarking on his second missionary journey with a new partner, Silas. As you read the account of Paul's journey to the town of Philippi, follow his route on a map and read his letter to the Philippians to get more of a feel for Paul's life with the people there. On Friday we move with Paul to Thessalonika, and you may want to read Paul's two letters to the Thessalonians as background. We leave Paul in Athens at the end of the week, realizing that he often met with failure as well as success in his missionary endeavors.

The Gospel readings:

The death of John the Baptist begins our week in Mark with a grim and foreboding feeling. John died for standing for the Word and truth of God in the face of evil. John's death points ahead to Jesus' death.

The familiar story of the Feeding of the Five Thousand is the appointed lesson for Tuesday. One of the beautiful images of the coming kingdom, or reign, of God prevalent in Jesus' time was the "messianic banquet." At the dawn of the new age, ". . . many will come from east and west and sit at table with Abraham, Isaac and Jacob in the kingdom of heaven. . ." (Matthew 8:11). The Lord will be the host at the banquet, and all peoples will feed and drink at the Lord's table. This feeding incident on the hillside can be seen as a foretaste of that banquet, just as the Eucharist is a foretaste of our life to come at the Lord's table in the kingdom. Notice the eucharistic-like words and actions in the description of Jesus taking the bread, breaking and blessing it, and then distributing it to the assembled people. Jesus comes to gather the family of God. Like the father of the Jewish home or the religious leader of a group of Jewish men, he blesses, breaks and distributes the bread in table fellowship as an expression of the people's relationship to the living God.

Feeding stories were not unique to Jesus. See 2 Kings 4:42-44 for a similar story told about the great prophet, Elisha. He, also, was remembered as having fed a group of people miraculously. People in Jesus' time would have connected Jesus with the great prophets of the Old Testament.

As you read Wednesday's lesson, your mind may move back to last Wednesday when we read that Jesus quieted the storm and the fears of the disciples, then came to shore to offer healing. This calming/healing motif is followed in today's reading, only this time the miracle of calming is heightened. Jesus is seen walking on water. He is about to pass the disciples by when he notices their fear. Again, Jesus exercises power over the elements by calming the storm. He walks over the waters that represented death and chaos to ancient peoples. Some scholars feel that this event may have actually been a resurrection appearance, but the power of the story in the early church lay in the hope that the event held out to a church living in confusion, persecution and fear. The Lord is in charge in this life as well as in the next. Even as the waters threaten to close over our heads, Christ walks with us in faith.

Think about St. Paul's controversy with the Jewish authorities as you read Thursday's lesson. Paul's insistence that gentiles could enter into relationship with Christ without following the strict dietary rituals of the orthodox Jew is given the authority of Jesus in these passages. It is not what goes into us that stands between us and holiness. It is what comes out of our lives that makes us holy in the sight of God. We dare not substitute empty ritual for life-giving service to the Lord. Realize the radical nature of these words as you read them. The ancient practices followed by generations of faithful Jews is questioned. Can we understand the reaction of the Jewish authorities in the face of Jesus' words and actions? How do we respond in church and nation to those who question the very heart of our actions and assumptions about life?

Notice the exhaustion of Jesus as you begin Friday's reading. Jesus would remove himself from the demands of the people, if only for a moment, but rest is impossible. A gentile woman places a demand on him for healing. Jesus' blunt words to her may shock us as we read them today: "Let the children first be fed, for it is not right to take the children's bread and throw it to the dogs." (Mark 7:27). The tone of Jesus' voice and the expression on his face are not seen or heard by us, but in any case, the woman throws his words back to him. Perhaps amused at her quickness, he responds to her request. Ironically, it is a woman considered by some "unfit to receive the children's bread" who shows the faith in Jesus that "the children" themselves lack. Perhaps it is the irony of this situation that causes Jesus to speak to the woman, using an expression of disdain applied to gentiles that was common in Jesus' time.

One healing is quickly followed by another, as the deaf and mute man comes to him. In contrast to the "dumb" people unable or unwilling to proclaim the new age that has dawned with Jesus, this "dumb" man now speaks. Isaiah's words come true: "On that day the deaf shall hear the words of a book, and out of their gloom and darkness the eyes of the blind shall see." (29:18).

You are not seeing double as you study Saturday's lesson. On Tuesday we read that Jesus fed 5,000 people, and now we read that Jesus fed 4,000 people, in a very similar account. Many scholars feel that this is simply a doublet, or repeating of the one story.

Week of the Sunday closest to August 3

The Old Testament readings:

The journey of the Ark into David's city of Jersualem continues in our reading Sunday. With ecstatic joy, David escorts the Ark. The Ark was not only of deep religious significance, but also a political symbol. It signified the uniting of the 12 tribes of Israel under the kingship of David, who would act in the name of the Lord who brought the Israelites out of Egypt, led them through the wilderness, and now brought them power and glory. Notice the painful words between David and his wife, Michal, daughter of Saul. With biting sarcasm, she ridicules his behavior before the people and points with disgust to the fact that "he exposed himself" before the slave girls of the town. Michal's anger is met by David's rejection of her from that moment on.

Now that the Ark is in Jerusalem, David wants to build a temple in which the Ark can be placed. Perhaps the prophet, Nathan, foresaw the dangers of such a temple. God can not be localized, he reminds David. He can not be confined to temple precincts. In later generations the presence of the Temple in Jerusalem did, indeed, give the people the feeling that the Lord would protect them no matter what their response to the covenant was. If the Temple was to be built, Nathan informed David, it would be built by his son. In fact, rather than David building a house for the Lord, the Lord would build a house for David. David's house would be his family, which would reign in Jerusalem for generations to come. The message of the Gospel is that Jesus, son of David, inherited this promise.

David continues to consolidate his power within the northern and southern tribes. His concern for Jonathan's remaining son, Mephibosheth, is a way of placating the followers of Saul, as well as a way of bringing honor to the memory of his friend.

The story of David and Bathsheba begins on Thursday. David succumbs to temptation, has intercourse with the wife of one of his military officers, and, when she is found to be pregnant, deliberately has her husband killed in battle to protect his name.

The prophet, Nathan, again confronts David with the Lord's word. In Nathan we see the role of the prophet. Nathan—and later Amos, Isaiah, Jeremiah, and the other prophets of Israel—interpreted the happenings of the day in the light of Israel's covenant with God. These prophets were not seers into the future as much as they were interpreters of the present. Note that David's sin may be forgiven, but the train of events that David's action began can not be reversed. The son born of Bathsheba dies, and David's household is filled with strife. The birth of Solomon would be a sign to David of a restored relationship with God, but it could not cancel out the price of his sinful act.

The Second readings:

On Monday we enter the city of Corinth with Paul. I'd suggest reading through 1 and 2 Corinthians as a background study of this era in Paul's life. The church in Corinth presented a great many problems to the apostle. You can feel his frustration and anger as you read those two letters.

Acts 18 gives us a thumbnail sketch of Paul's missionary method. Notice that he joins with others in Corinth who follow his trade of tentmaking and works to support himself. (This is the origin of the term, "tentmaking ministry" describing the ministry of deacons and priests who earn their income from work outside the church.) Paul then preaches to the Jews within the synagogue community. After being rejected there, he moves right next door to begin his work among the gentiles. Is it any wonder that Paul is roundly hated by the Jews in the towns where he works? Lest we condemn the Jews of Paul's time too harshly, we need to put ourselves in their shoes as we read these passages.

Mid-week we move with Paul back to Antioch (Acts 18:22-23) where he sets out on his third missionary journey, which includes major work in the city of Ephesus.

The Gospel readings:

Monday's and Tuesday's readings contrast being blind and

58

having true sight. The Pharisees demand a sign from Jesus who denies that God would send signs "in this generation." The disciples, however, have been seeing signs all around them as they follow Jesus, especially in the miracle of the loaves! Despite the signs, they remain blind to their significance.

The reference to yeast, or leaven, found in the reading was a common metaphor. Evil rises up in life, infecting all of society, just as yeast rises up in dough. (This explains why yeast, a metaphor for evil, is removed from Jewish households at the time of Passover to this day.)

We read of the healing of the blind man at Bethsaida. The blind man can now see far more clearly than those blind disciples! Real sight begins to come to Peter, however, as he realizes who Jesus is, but he still cannot see as God would have him see. He cannot see that Jesus as Messiah must suffer and die.

This passage marks the hinge point of the Gospel of Mark. From this point on in our daily reading of Mark, our faces will be set toward Jerusalem as Jesus moves toward his destiny.

The collect for Friday, on page 99 of the Book of Common Prayer, sets the theme for Wednesday's reading:

> Almighty God, whose most dear Son went not up to joy but first he suffered pain, and entered not into glory before he was crucified; Mercifully grant that we, walking in the way of the cross, may find it none other than the way of life and of peace.

The disciples of Jesus must bear the cross in every age, words that stand in stark contrast to the assumption that when one follows Jesus life will be peaceful and profitable.

On Thursday you may want to look back to Exodus 24:1-18 for background to appreciate the significance of the transfiguration. Moses went "up into a cloud" to receive the Law from the Lord. Jesus takes Peter, James and John with him "up into the mountain" for a revelation of the new Law which is Jesus, a law not written on stone, but written on the hearts of the people. (See Jeremiah 31:31).

Several other points need to be kept in mind: Elijah was the great prophet of Israel who lived in the time of King Ahab and Queen Jezebel (1 Kings). Tradition held that it would be Elijah who would return at the coming of the Messiah to herald the day of the Lord. The Feast of Booths was a joyous fall harvest festival in which shelters were erected from harvest stalks and vines to celebrate God's presence with the people as they wandered in the wilderness. According to Zechariah 14:16-19 all nations would celebrate that feast together at the coming of the final day of the Lord. Peter's mention of the tent, or booth, or tabernacle is a reference to that great expectation. Tradition held that Elijah's role at the ushering in of the day of the Lord was to purify the people of God, to turn them back to Torah. Jesus saw this as the role of John the Baptist, who had already come and been killed by Herod. Jesus was not to be confused with Elijah. He was to be the suffering servant of the Lord, the servant who would die so that healing and salvation might come for all people.

When Moses came down from the mountain after receiving the tablets of the Law, he was immediately met with confusion and loss of faith on the part of the people (Exodus 32). In his absence, they had created a golden calf to worship. Now as Jesus comes down from the "Mountain of Revelation" he, also, meets with the loss of faith and confusion among his disciples. No wonder his anguished words: "How long must I put up with this people?"

Week of the Sunday closest to August 10

The Old Testament readings:

This week we follow the tragic story of the strife within David's family that Nathan had warned of when he confronted the king. Though David is a mighty king and warrior, when it comes to his own family his blind love for his sons leads to indecision, resulting in power struggles in the family.

The tragedy begins with Sunday's reading. David's eldest son, Amnon, rapes his half-sister, Tamar, who is the sister of David's second oldest son, Absalom. Not only are we dealing with the feelings of hatred and anger between the brothers caused by the rape of Tamar, but also with the rivalry for their father's throne. In your reading notice that David takes no direct action, either in connection with the rape or the resultant murder of his eldest son. David seems unable to respond with strength when it comes to dealing with his own sons.

Remember Nathan's parable told to David after his marriage to Bathsheba? When David pronounced judgment on the rich neighbor, he was pronouncing his own judgment. Joab arranges for a similar confrontation with David. When David speaks of the need for protection for a woman's son, David is forced to acknowledge the need for reconciliation with his own son.

No sooner is Absalom restored to his father than he immediately begins positioning himself for power against his father. Each day he appears at the city gate to undercut his father's judgment. He cleverly plays on the feelings of people from the northern tribal regions where Saul has come from, in order to establish a power base with them. Absalom is a politically astute man. Hebron is a good place to stir up the revolt. He was born there, and it was David's place of residence and rule for seven years. There could have been jealousy within the area over David's choice of Jerusalem as his capital.

On Friday and Saturday we read the details of David's departure from Jerusalem as Absalom's army prepares to drive him out. Picture in your mind refugees leaving cities that are about to be invaded by an enemy, only in this case the enemy is

David's own son, Absalom. We read of David's loyal followers encouraging him in his sad trek out of the city. Even Ittai the Gittite, a mercenary soldier from an alien land who has just arrived in Jerusalem, chooses to follow the king into exile. Notice the spy network that David leaves behind and note that he refuses to remove the Ark of the Covenant from the city. Keep your eye on Ahithophel, a man whose word is always listened to when he speaks in David's court. Now he chooses to leave David and join the rebellion.

Ziba is a character you will meet for the second time in Saturday's reading. He was a servant of Saul's who told David about Jonathan's son, Mephibosheth, when David wanted to protect Jonathan's family. Now Ziba is one who supports David on the road, while Mephibosheth is one who seems to go over to the rebellion.

The Second readings:

Last week we read that Paul, like Jesus, was determined to return to Jerusalem. He knew his visit would be dangerous, but he felt compelled to go. His ultimate dream was to carry the Gospel to Rome.

After leaving Ephesus, he travels through Greece to encourage the churches there and to continue the work of spreading the Gospel. He then starts eastward toward Jerusalem. Notice on Monday the touching farewell scene with the elders from Ephesus who met him at Miletus. Ironically, it is Paul's Roman citizenship that saves him from his own people when he is arrested in Jerusalem. Remember, an overriding message in Acts reminds us time and again that nothing can stop the spread of the Gospel. Now the Roman Empire will be the vehicle that Paul uses to reach Rome itself. He will have the opportunity to appear before people of influence in the Roman hierarchy.

The Gospel readings:

To appreciate fully this week's readings from the Gospel of Mark, picture the church to whom this gospel is addressed.

It is a church under persecution. The converts have been promised eternal life in the risen Christ, but they are now experiencing martyrdom, ridicule, rejection and suffering. It is into this painful situation that the Gospel of Mark is written. This section of Mark, starting with Mark 8:34 and continuing through the end of chapter 10, is a teaching section for new converts and for the church in general. "This is what it means to be a follower of the risen Christ," Mark is saying. "This is what you can expect out of your discipleship."

Monday's reading speaks strong words for the church. The "little ones," or recent converts, must not be tempted to forego the Gospel for the sake of present comfort. To tempt the weak is to invite instant condemnation for yourself. Temptation to sin must be resisted at all costs. The closing words for Monday warn the Christian that being tested by "salt and fire" is part of what life-in-Christ means. The Christian is to "salt," or flavor, the environment. Tasteless salt is worthless.

Marriage and divorce with the Christian covenant is the focus for Tuesday's readings. Jesus' words seem restrictive in our age when divorce is recognized by the church. Remember that in Jesus' day wives could be easily divorced by their husbands; wives had very few rights of their own. Jesus' teaching on divorce protects the woman and affirms her status in her husband's house. Historically, the church has exercised the privilege of modifying Jesus' teaching in the light of the guidance of the Holy Spirit. Matthew 18:18 has been seen as the authority for this interpretive aspect of the church's life: "Truly, I say to you, whatever you bind on earth shall be bound in heaven, and whatever you loose on earth shall be loosed in heaven."

Jesus' words read on Wednesday are harsh. It is impossible for the rich and powerful to enter into the kingdom of God. We try to modify those words and set them aside in our extremely affluent culture, but Jesus saw clearly that it was the poor and powerless who responded to his words, his healings, and his presence. These were the people who knew their dependence on God. The church, during the time the written gospels were developed, experienced the same phenomena. It was the poor and the oppressed who responded to the Gospel. No wonder the writer of the Book of the Acts of the Apostles explained that converts sold all their possessions and shared what they had equally as each person had need. There will be a complete reversal of life when God's reign comes. The "first shall be last" and the "last shall be first" is a common theme throughout the New Testament.

Discipleship also results in a reversal of expectations, we learn on Thursday. James and John expect reward and prestige; instead, they will receive the cup and baptism of martyrdom. One who is a disciple is one who serves, rather than one who is served. Think of the impact of those words on a church suffering from persecution. Think of the impact of the words on the church in Poland, Central America and other places where Christians suffer for their faith and their convictions.

Each day in our reading we move closer to Jerusalem. Friday's walk with Christ brings us to Jericho, 12 hard, uphill hours from the great city. Through faith, Bartimaeus, whom Jesus meets outside of Jericho, receives his sight.

We move out of the teaching, or catechetical, section of Mark's Gospel on Saturday as we stand with the crowds who greet Jesus on his triumphal entry into Jerusalem. In order to appreciate this traditional Palm Sunday passage, you need to keep a few facts in mind: The horse was a beast of war and conquest, while the ass was a sign of peace. When a king came on an ass, it meant he came to announce a reign of peace and justice. The spreading of garments and branches on the ground was an ancient sign of greeting to the king. (See 2 Kings 9:13 for an Old Testament example of this custom.) At the great Jewish festival of Tabernacles (also called the Feast of Booths) and again at the time of Hannukah, branches were waved and words from Psalm 118:25-26 were shouted by the people. Hannukah celebrated the rededication of the Temple by the Jews at the time the Greeks were driven out in 164 B.C. The Feast of Booths was celebrated as an annual renewal of the covenant between God and the nation. It was also a time of recalling the years of wilderness pilgrimage in which God led them toward the Promised Land. One of the images of the coming reign of God was that all nations would join the Jews in Jerusalem for the great Feast of Tabernacles. (See Zechariah 14:16-21). All nations will keep the covenant celebrated by the Jews at this great pilgrimage festival.

"Hosanna" meant "Save now!" in Hebrew. As we reflect on the ancient traditions associated with Jesus' entry into Jerusalem, we can see both the political and religious impact of his action. In a sense, Jesus was acting out a living parable of his life and death among the people.

Week of the Sunday closest to August 17

The Old Testament readings:

The painful story of Absalom's revolt continues this week. David's carefully laid-out spy network is a successful operation, we discover on Sunday. Remember Hushai from last week's reading? He was the man we read about Friday who wanted to follow David into exile, but was ordered to stay behind and play the role of double agent. Now he is able to counteract the advice of Athithophel, who urges Absalom to pursue David and his army immediately. If Absalom had followed that advice, he might well have won the day.

Mahanaim, a city some distance northeast of Jerusalem in the territory of Gilead, is David's base camp. Help and reinforcements come to him there. He watches his army move out of the city to do battle with his son. What a poignant moment for this great king and commander. Amasa is appointed commander of Absalom's army.

Last week we heard of Absalom's great head of hair. Perhaps it is his hair that is his undoing. While he sees his army routed in defeat, he is somehow caught in the compromising position of hanging from a tree by his head.

And now, more tragedy for the king. News of his son's death comes to him and his grief overwhelms any sense of victory. By Thursday we will be reading of David's triumphant return to the city he fled a short time ago. Even Shimei, who shouted denunciations at the king earlier, is forgiven by David in this moment of victory. Note that Amasa is placed in charge of David's army as a means of punishing Joab for Absalom's death and, perhaps, as a political move to gain the allegiance of Absalom's followers.

On Friday we get a hint of things to come between the northern tribes of Israel and the southern tribes of Judah. David comes from Judah. Saul's roots lie in Israel. On David's return, jealousy springs up between the northerners and the southerners, a sense of discord that leads later to civil war between the two halves of David's kingdom. Remember Jonathan's son,

Mephibosheth, whom David took into his court? Last week we learned that Ziba, who had discovered Saul's crippled grandson in the first place, had informed David that Mephibosheth had decided to align himself with Absalom. Notice the encounter between king and former court companion.

We'll be jumping over some narrative material between Friday and Saturday's readings. Sheba starts a rebellion against David among the people of Israel, again pointing to the split in David's kingdom that comes some years later. One rebellion leads immediately to another. There is to be no peace for David even within his own kingdom. We move on Saturday to 2 Samuel 23, part of a loose collection of stories, psalms and conclusions about David's reign that are placed together in the last four chapters of the book. The "last words of David" is simply a psalm attributed to David to give a flavor of how he viewed life as God's servant. The story of David at battle asking for water from Bethlehem, his place of birth, is simply told to add insight about the kind of leader David was.

The Second readings:

Our adventures in the Acts of the Apostles continue through this week and next. Paul's captivity drags on as first one governor and then another are not quite sure how to handle his case. The governors' desire to keep favor with the Jews keeps them from releasing Paul, and he languishes in jail for over two years in Caesarea. But Paul has limited freedom to talk with his followers and to encourage them. The imprisonment and court hearing provide Paul with excellent opportunities to preach the Gospel before important Roman authorities. Paul finally appeals to Caesar to avoid being turned over to the religious authorities in Jerusalem.

The Gospel readings:

On Monday we read the events thought to have happened on the Monday of what we today call Holy Week. It is now the "next day" after the triumphal entry, and Jesus again enters the city after spending the night at Bethany, a town about

1¾ miles from Jerusalem. The curse of the fig tree can best be understood as a parable told by Jesus (see Luke 13:6-9) that the writer of Mark placed in the narrative to emphasize the point of what was happening in these final days.

A little background is necessary to appreciate the cleansing-of-the-Temple scene. Jesus is not upset with the money-changing and selling going on in the Temple. That is essential for the carrying on of the rites of Judaism. It is the unfair practices that have grown up around the money-changing and sale of sacrificial animals that arouse his anger. But of more importance, Jesus is acting out a prophetic drama to make a clear statement to the people that he is announcing the inauguration of the messianic age. Take a moment now and read Jeremiah 7:1-16, Isaiah 56:7 and Malachi 3:3-5 so that you can see Jesus' activity here through the same perspective as the people of his time. You may also want to read Jeremiah 13:1-11 and Isaiah 20:1-6 for examples of similar dramatic actions by the prophets.

Jesus' actions at the Temple are not lost on the authorities. They move quickly to entrap him in order to discredit him among the people and to find grounds on which he can be brought before the Jewish and Roman courts.

Wednesday's reference to paying taxes is not meant to imply that there are two separated realms of responsibility in the world, the sacred and the secular. The "things that are God's" are everything in heaven and earth, if we take the Torah seriously. The closing words on Wednesday are subtle. (Mark 12:26-27). If God identified himself to Moses at the burning bush as "I am the God of Abraham" rather than "I was the God of Abraham," surely that indicated that Abraham still had a living relationship with God.

Thursday you will read familiar words from the Book of Common Prayer in Mark 12:29-31:

> . . .'Hear, O Israel: The Lord our God, the Lord is one; and you shall love the Lord your God with all your heart, and with all your soul, and with all your mind, and with all your strength.' The second is this, 'You shall love your

neighbor as yourself.' There is no other commandment greater than these.

Note that these are not Jesus' own words; he quotes from the Torah (first five books of the Old Testament), from Deuteronomy 6:4-5 and Leviticus 19:18.

The opening words on Friday (Mark 12:35-36) can be confusing as Jesus is again making subtle use of scripture to prove his point. The Messiah was to be more than a military hero, more than a descendant of David. He would, indeed, be one called Lord, one who would stand far above kings, prophets, priests, or people. "Enlarge your vision of the Messiah," Jesus is saying in this rather obscure passage.

Chapter 13 of Mark is a collection of Jesus' sayings and parables about the final times that would come before the new age was ushered in. If you want to overwhelm your friends or Bible study companions, call this the "eschatological discourse." Eschatology is a technical term in theology meaning the "last things" of life, from the Greek word meaning last or extreme. Those "last times" will be soon, Jesus warns, and yet he modifies that expectation with the comment in Mark 13:10—"And the Gospel must first be preached to all nations." Struggle and persecution are seen by Jesus as a part of those final times. Certainly as Mark's readers faced their own persecution for the Gospel, they would have had Jesus' words firmly in mind.

Week of the Sunday closest to August 24

The Old Testament readings:

Our reading of 2 Samuel is concluded on Sunday with a rather strange story of David's census and God's anger over that act. First, the text states that the Lord ordered a census, but then the Lord proceeded to punish David for the act. It is not clear why the census was seen as an act that would anger God, though it could have been perceived as a lack of faith on David's part. It was the kind of action despotic kings took as they counted their people for military duty and forced labor.

The importance of the story lies in the fact that the threshing floor on which David offered sacrifice was the site where the Temple was eventually built. You will need to keep this detail in mind for your reading later in the week. The harsh punishment meted out by God and the sight of the avenging angel should be read with the narrator's theological perspective in mind as well. When the nation suffered, divine punishment was the reason. Thus, a severe epidemic coming shortly after a census would be perceived by king and prophet alike as a direct action of God.

On Monday we begin the reading of 1 Kings. Though our assigned reading does not begin until verse 5 of chapter 1, I'd suggest you begin with the first verse. Our once noble and mighty warrior king is now a senile old man who must have a young woman wait on him and keep him warm at night. What a tragic scene of impending death. Notice the parenthetical statement in 1 Kings 1:6: "His father had never at any time displeased him (David's son, Adonijah) by asking, 'Why have you done thus and so?'" David never corrected his sons. How well we know that by now!

We meet King Solomon on Wednesday. His entrance on the stage of salvation history begins with a dream in which he asks God for wisdom, rather than wealth or long life. The Lord rewards him accordingly with wealth, power, influence *and* the wisdom he sought.

The Temple will finally be built, we discover on Friday. A foreign king aids in the project, one familiar with the construction of sacred places and who has resources—skilled engineers and laborers. Solomon is not above using forced labor from among his own people for his building projects, you will notice. David's census perhaps helps him in this endeavor. The cruel actions of David's son lead toward the rebellion of the northern tribes that come on Solomon's death.

Remember the great day when David brought the Ark into Jerusalem? (The week of proper 13). Now the scene is repeated with even greater triumph and splendor. The Ark of the Covenant is carried to the Temple and placed within its walls. 1 Kings 8:12-13 expresses the theological understanding of this act. The God known in the wilderness wandering days and in the early days of the settlement in the Promised Land had always been perceived as moving with the people. He led the Hebrews by cloud and fire through the wilderness. With the building of the Temple, God is now perceived as inhabiting that specific place. To be near God is to be at the Temple in Jerusalem. The great pilgrimage festivals of Israel retell that understanding. Years later when the people are exiled to Babylonia this localized understanding of God will present a major theological crisis. (See Psalm 137). The prophets of the exile help to enlarge the vision of the people. God is beyond the walls of any Temple. God dwells with a people in exile. The Lord is a God of heaven and earth.

The great celebration probably came during the Feast of Tabernacles (month of Ethanim). God was "brought" into the Temple at this great time of pilgrimage celebration, the Jewish people would remember in the coming generations. Think back to last week's reading of Jesus' triumphant entry into Jerusalem; some scholars feel that Jesus' entry happened at the Feast of Tabernacles rather than the Passover. In any case, the traditions of Tabernacles were followed in the way Jesus was greeted. Can you see the impact of Jesus' action? "Yes, the Lord is again coming into his Temple, just as the Lord was brought into the Temple in Solomon's time. See, it is *my* Temple. I have the right to purify it." No wonder Jesus was crucified!

The Second readings:

We conclude our reading of Acts this week. Paul approaches Rome, a city he has longed to visit. His captivity serves to increase his opportunities to heal and to preach the Gospel. Nothing can stop the spread of the Good News, the writer of Acts reminds us with each account of Paul's activities.

The book ends in mystery. We do not know what happened to Paul after his two years of virtual house arrest. Church tradition says he was martyred in Rome, but there is a hint from the closing verses of Acts that Paul may have been freed, at least for a time. Chapter 28:30-31 describes the "two whole years" of his captivity with no reference to a trial or martyrdom. In any case, it is clear that Paul exercised his ministry in every possible way. Whatever happened, Paul was a living witness to the risen Christ through the power of the Holy Spirit.

The Gospel readings:

Jesus foresees the terrible destruction of Jerusalem by the Romans that will come after his death. In 70 A.D. the Romans responded to a Jewish rebellion by destroying the Temple and the holy city. Jesus senses that coming conflict and confrontation. He sees it as a sign that the new age of God is dawning. Out of the ashes of the old the new kingdom of God will be built. The Temple in Jerusalem will be replaced by the living temple that is Jesus' presence in the world. (The indwelling of the Holy Spirit in the lives of the people will make each person a living temple of the Lord, St. Paul said in later years. See 1 Corinthians 6:19.) Jesus uses the language of apocalypticism, a highly poetic and symbolic language of hope for a people living in an age of persecution and oppression. Read Daniel 12:1-3 for a flavor of this style of literature. The thrust of the message is that God is soon going to intervene to bring the present age of darkness to an end and usher in a new age of the Lord.

The Last Supper becomes our focus on Thursday. You must keep in mind the traditions of the Jewish Passover to understand the implications of this meal with the disciples. As usual,

Jesus takes the traditions of his people and forges new meaning out of the familiar. Realize that lambs were slaughtered at the Passover as a sacrifice for the sins of the people. Each family would buy an unblemished lamb at the Temple grounds. The sins of the family would be laid on the lamb, and then the priests would slaughter the lamb. Its blood would be poured on the altar and the family's sins would be washed away. It is within this context that we see Jesus as the "Lamb of God, that takest away the sins of the world." The lamb was eaten at the Passover meal, but now Jesus' Body, the bread, is broken and eaten as thanksgiving (in the Greek language, "eucharist"). He is the sacrifice. The cup of wine traditionally shared at the Passover meal as the "cup of affliction" becomes for the faithful the blood of Christ that cleanses and reconciles the people with God as no sacrificial lamb's blood can do. Moreover, Jesus' blood seals the new covenant as the blood of sacrificial animals sealed the old covenant between God and our people of the wilderness. (See Exodus 24:8).

One other important image needs to be understood here. When Jesus says (Mark 14:25), "Truly, I say to you, I shall not drink again of the fruit of the vine until that day when I drink it new in the kingdom of God," he is referring to the messianic banquet.

> On this mountain the Lord of hosts will make for all peoples a feast of fat things, a feast of wine on the lees, of fat things full of marrow, of wine on the lees well refined. And he will destroy on this mountain the covering that is cast over all peoples, the veil that is spread over all nations. (Isaiah 25:6-7).

The Eucharist is a foretaste of that banquet. We step "into" the kingdom of God each time we share the Eucharist. We gather at the banquet table today knowing that, as we do so, we are getting our "first course" in the banquet that is to come.

Moreover, we join at the Eucharist with all those who have gone before and sing one great triumphant hymn of praise "with Angels, and Archangels and all the company of heaven." (BCP, p. 362).

Week of the Sunday closest to August 31

The Old Testament readings:

We read Solomon's prayer to God at the time of the dedication of the Temple as we begin our week in the Old Testament. The theological question I discussed last week about God being perceived as "dwelling" within the confines of the Temple is raised in the prayer. "But will God indeed dwell on the earth?" (1 Kings 8:27). It is important to realize that much of what we read here is not verbatim quotations from Solomon, but rather reflects the historical developments that came long after Solomon. Most of 1 Kings was written during our peoples' exile in Babylonia after the destruction of the Temple and the city of Jerusalem. The people of that time remembered the understanding of their ancestors that God dwelled in the Temple. The writer of 1 Kings was careful to point out that God was far too powerful and omnipotent to dwell anywhere.

On Monday we move for a moment into 2 Chronicles, a book written after the Babylonian exile. Chronicles is a very idealized historical survey of Judah from the time of David to the Babylonian exile. The books of Ezra and Nehemiah were written by the same school of writers. Their point in writing the historical survey was to encourage the returned exiles in their dedication to Temple worship and to the restoration of their role in history as a holy nation of covenanted people. The narrative parallels the historical survey found in Samuel and Kings. Today's reading is the chronicler's version of Solomon's prayer of consecration of the Temple. Note 2 Chronicles 6:40: "Now, O my God, let thy eyes be open and thy ears attentive to a prayer of this place." This is a one- sentence description of the role of the Temple in the lives of the people. Notice, also, the next verse: ". . .and let thy priest . . .be clothed with salvation. . ."—the origin of one of the suffrages said at Morning and Evening Prayer. (See BCP, p. 97). The Feast of Tabernacles ends, we read on Tuesday, and the people who have gathered for the consecration of the temple leave for home. The rather simplistic theological perspective of the writer of 1 and 2 Kings is set forth in Tuesday's reading. The king and nation will succeed so long as they follow their covenant with God.

First, we hear of Solomon's great power and wisdom. Even the Queen of Sheba is amazed at his wisdom and power. The Millo referred to in Wednesday's reading was part of the fortifications of the city. From praise we turn to condemnation. Thursday's reading is filled with foreboding. Solomon, it would appear, loves women more than God! Foreign wives mean the worship of foreign gods. As punishment, the region of the northern 10 tribes (Israel) will be torn away from Solomon. The somber word to Solomon is soon put into play when the prophet, Ahijah, meets Jeroboam on the road. The prophet tears Jeroboam's cloak into 12 pieces and gives him 10 as a sign that the 10 northern tribes will be governed by Jeroboam rather than Solomon's son, Rehoboam. This grim sign of a divided nation becomes an actual fact when Rehoboam meets with the northern tribes after Solomon's death. Rehoboam is no politician. Rather than promising the easing of the burden of enforced labor and other oppressive measures, he promises an even stronger hand against the northern tribes. The taunting song in Saturday's reading—"What portion have we in David?" (1 Kings 12:16)—expresses the disdain for David's family line. The once great nation moulded and shaped by Saul and David and strengthened by Solomon is now to be split into two weaker kingdoms. Israel includes the former territories of the 10 northern tribes and Judah encompasses the tribal area of Judah and Simeon. David's descendants continue to hold power in Judah, but now a new order of kings takes the throne of the northern kingdom.

The Epistle readings:

This week we read a Letter of James beginning our sequential reading with chapter 2. Scholars disagree over whether this letter was actually written by James, the brother of Jesus, or by a writer who lived later in the first century, or even early in the second century. Because the letter is addressed to the problems of a well established church, a later dating would seem more plausible.

Though the first chapter is not assigned in the lectionary, take a few extra moments on Monday and read it. We are to be doers of the word, and not just hearers, we read. Look at this definition at the end of chapter 1: "Religion that is pure and undefiled before God and the Father is this: to visit orphans and widows in their affliction, and to keep oneself unstained from the world." (James 1:27).

Social justice and compassion for the poor and the oppressed are the marks of a faithful person, James points out. "So faith by itself, if it has no works, is dead." (James 2:17). Then he goes on to outline what an active faith looks like in the Christian community. Faith shapes values and relationships and moves people to respond to the needs of others in the community. Faith calls the wealthy to task because they place reliance on themselves and tend to oppress their workers in order to gain more. Saturday's reading includes the call to lay hands on the sick and to confess sins to one another. Prayer and confession lead to healing and wholeness in the Body of Christ.

The Gospel readings:

This week in midsummer may feel like Holy Week to you as you read the story of the passion of our Lord. The story is familiar, of course. I'll comment on just a point.

The three hours of darkness mentioned by Mark probably reflects his theological view of this moment more than an actual historic event. The ninth plague that came to the Egyptians before our biblical ancestors left Egypt at the exodus was darkness. (See Exodus 10:22). In Isaiah 13:10 and Joel 2:10 the prophets both talk about darkness and the failure of the sun as a sign that the day of the Lord has come, a day of judgment and vengeance for the wicked. Surely this moment at Jesus' death was the day of the Lord, the announcement of the kingdom of God and a day of judgment for the world as well.

Week of the Sunday closest to September 7

The Old Testament readings:

You will need a score card to keep track of the players during these weeks we'll spend in 1 and 2 Kings. We've got two lines of kings reigning simultaneously now, since Israel and Judah are split. The biblical writers identify the reign of Israel's kings by their counterparts' reigns in Judah and vice versa. This can be confusing unless you keep in front of you a biblical time chart that lists the kings.

Jeroboam, the first king of the northern kingdom of Israel, needed to establish his political and religious supremacy. The last thing he wanted was people treking down to the Temple at Jerusalem for the three great pilgrimage festivals each year. Jerusalem not only symbolized the presence of God for the people, it also reminded the people of David and his sons. To counteract that strong religious and political pull, one of Jeroboam's first acts was to establish altars to God at Dan in the north and at Bethel, a city that lay conveniently on the way to Jerusalem. Pilgrimage festivals were quickly instituted by Jeroboam to rival the pilgrimage festivals in Jerusalem. Though the text mentions golden calves, these may simply have been thrones upon which the Lord would symbolically "sit," rather than rival gods. Bethel had been a place of pilgrimage for the people of Israel way back in the time of the partiarchs. Dan was a new shrine, but it, too, had legitimacy with the people. Jeroboam's capital city was Shechem.

Monday's reading is the kind of story that would have been told by the people of the southern kingdom to point out how evil Jeroboam's rival altars were in the mind of the Lord.

On Tuesday, after skipping over several chapters, we meet King Omri. Omri, commander in chief of the army, was proclaimed king by his troops in the field. His predecessor had ruled for just seven days. It was a time of upheaval and unrest. Despite the short shrift given Omri by the writer of our narration, Omri was truly a great king who brought stability and some degree of power back to the northern kingdom of Israel.

One of his acts was to establish the city of Samaria as his capital. Later, the whole area would be called Samaria. Now we see the origins of some of the animosity between the Jews and the Samaritans so evident in Jesus' time.

The years of Omri's reign were 885-874 B.C. Notice the refrain in connection with Omri: "Omri did what was evil in the sight of the Lord and did more evil than all who were before him." (1 Kings 16:25). This will be an increasingly familiar refrain after a few more weeks in 1 and 2 Kings. The downfall of the northern and southern kingdoms came, according to the deuteronomic schools of writers, because of the decadence of the kings. The Book of the Chronicles of the Kings of Israel, mentioned several times in the text, was apparently an official court record that has long since been lost.

Tuesday is a big day, for Elijah comes on the scene, the great prophet mentioned so often in the gospels in connection with Jesus and John the Baptist. We also meet King Ahab, who ruled from 874 to 853 B.C. His wife, Jezebel, was a wicked woman from Phoenicia whom Ahab married for political reasons. She brought foreign religious practices and ruthless patterns of leadership into the political life of Israel.

For the rest of the week we read stories about Elijah's struggle to neutralize Ahab's and Jezebel's evil influence over Israel. The worship practices Jezebel brought with her from Phoenicia infuriated Elijah. Enjoy the Elijah stories as the kind of stories families shared around the evening meal for generations.

Friday's reading ridicules the priests of Baal who were supported by Jezebel. During a competitive sacrifice with the priests of Baal, Elijah mimics their ecstatic dancing and shouting. He taunts them, suggesting that their god is asleep or too busy to accept their offering. When it is Elijah's turn to offer sacrifice to Yahweh, he pours water over the sacrifice to heighten the miracle of fire.

From great victory over the priests of Baal, Elijah quickly moves to despair as Jezebel threatens his life. The 40 days' journey he takes to Mt. Horeb is meant to remind us of Moses' 40 days on the mountain with the Lord.

The Epistle readings:

We read Paul's letter to the church at Philippi this week. If you want some background on Paul's life among the Philippians, read Acts 16:11-40. Opinions among scholars vary as to where Paul was when he wrote the letter to the Philippians. He could have written it from a prison cell at Ephesus or at Rome, where he was held under house arrest for some time. In any case, this letter was written during a time of great stress. Despite his imprisonment, Paul wrote with a sense of joy and gratitude for what the Philippians had done to support him and for their growing faith in the Lord. His only concern was that he had heard there were some in their group who were trying to convince them that they must adopt the strict ritualistic provisions of the Jews in order to be followers of Christ. Paul warned his friends to avoid such demands. Christ had brought them a new covenant. They were not to fall back into the practices of the old covenant.

Philippians 2:6-11 is probably an ancient liturgical hymn or creed taken right out of early Christian worship life and inserted here by Paul.

Philippians 2:12 may be familiar to you: ". . .work out your own salvation with fear and trembling," along with Philippians 3:10 which reads, "All I care for is to know Christ, to experience the power of his resurrection, and to share his sufferings, in growing conformity with his death if only I may finally arrive at the resurrection from the dead." (New English Bible). Our reading of Philippians ends with another familiar passage, often used in connection with the blessing offered at the Eucharist: "And the peace of God, which passes all understanding, will keep your hearts and your minds in Christ Jesus." (4:7).

The Gospel readings:

Many scholars over the years have felt that the last verses of Mark, assigned as an option in our daily lectionary, were added to the gospel in late New Testament times. Thus the empty tomb, rather than the resurrection, crowns Mark's gospel.

As the new school year begins so does our reading of the

Gospel of Matthew. This gospel was written later than Mark. Where Mark's gospel was written to strengthen a young church suffering persecution, Matthew's was written to provide instruction for a young church beginning to face reality that the faithful Christian must live for a period of time in the world before the return of the Lord at the end of the age. How were they to understand their life in Christ in that age? Who had authority in the church? How were decisions to be made? How was the covenant revealed through Christ to direct their daily lives? How could they explain their faith in Christ to their friends? Matthew, though written after the Gospel of Mark, comes first in the order of the gospels because it sets the tone for the teaching and authority of the church.

The stories we read at the end of this week are familiar. The Magi coming with gifts establish Jesus' authority as the expected Messiah, the "king of the Jews." Notice they visit Jesus in a house, not in a lowly stable. We find a distinctly different birth narrative than Luke's, one that concentrates on the royalty of Jesus as one who came as a descendant of King David. Jesus is the new Israel, who in his infancy follows the path of the first Israel. Mary, Joseph and Jesus go down into Egypt and return the same way, through the wilderness, that their ancestors took at the time of the Exodus. These early stories in Matthew serve more as an overture in narrative form than an accurate historical account of the Lord's infancy.

Matthew's term, "kingdom of heaven," denotes the breaking of the new age into the present age. Heaven denotes a radically new reality that turns history and creation upside down as God works to redeem life as well as death.

The Sermon on the Mount will be our focus for the last part of the week. The writer of the gospel collected many of Jesus' sayings and placed them together in this first of five great teaching discourses. Here Jesus instructs his disciples on the way of righteousness. Matthew constantly reinforced the theme that Jesus brought the new covenant. Matthew did this in an almost subliminal way by lining up Jesus' actions against the backdrop of the liberation pilgrimage that Moses and the Israelites made from Egyptian slavery to the Promised Land. Just as Moses went up in the mountain to offer the Law, so Jesus goes up on a mountain to instruct his disciples in the new Law. Jesus is a new lawgiver. This is, indeed, the new covenant or the new testament.

Read Isaiah 61:1-2 for the context out of which Jesus spoke the Beatitudes. The Lord comes to the powerless, to the struggling peoples who know they cannot live by their own power. He comes to those seeking what is right and who are ready actively to oppose what is unjust in society. Those who are now struggling and seeking will be fulfilled in the reign of God. Indeed, they already taste that fulfillment as they sit on the hillside with Jesus.

Matthew 5:17-20 sets the record straight. Jesus did not come to negate the Law and the Prophets. He came to fulfill them. The Torah was felt by the faithful Jew to be the perfect revelation of wisdom to all people. Jesus did not deny the wisdom of the Law. He announced that he had come to deepen the revelation, to move beyond the teaching of Torah. His own life would be a living experience of what the Torah stated in writing. With Jesus, Torah was incarnate, lived out in flesh and blood.

Week of the Sunday closest to September 14

The Old Testament readings:

The encounter on Mt. Horeb between God and Elijah opens our week in 1 Kings. Think back to the theophany (appearance of God) that came on this mountain when the Israelites gathered with Moses to receive the covenant. The wind and earthquake are reminiscent of that crucial moment in our peoples' history, but today the word of the Lord comes to Elijah in the stillness that follows earthquake and fire. Elijah speaks like a child to a parent: "I'm the only one faithful." The Lord is not patient with Elijah's feelings of despair. Elijah is not the only faithful one left. There are 7,000 others ready to rise up. It is revolution that calls Elijah back into the struggle. The Lord is acting in history, and Elijah must be a part of that action. As we attempt to keep the church at a safe distance from the struggles of nation and society in our day, we need to remember the strong words of the Lord to Elijah.

Monday and Tuesday we read of the encounters between prophet and king. Notice the role of prophet set forth here. The prophet speaks God's word to the king, a word that confronted the evil actions of the royal household. There can be no compromising the covenant law of justice. God is just and holy. God's people and God's kings must be just and holy. The church is called to carry on the role of prophet in society, standing for the oppressed and demanding justice. This sacred calling often puts the church at odds with the authorities of our own age.

There are always court prophets who will speak the words the civil authorities want to hear. Micaiah is not such a prophet. He speaks the word of God which put him into direct conflict with the king. God's word cannot be equated with the words and will of men and women nor the state that governs them. Isaiah stated the awesome distance between God's word and the word of men and women well when he said,

'For my thoughts are not your thoughts, neither are your ways my ways,' says the Lord. 'For as the heavens are higher than the earth, so are my ways higher than your ways and my thoughts than your thoughts.' (Isaiah 55:8-9).

The state would shape the Lord's word to fit political expediency. The church today must look to Micaiah as the one who models the response of the church to civil authorities of our day.

A new king comes to the throne in our Friday reading. Ahaziah, the son of Ahab, became king in about 853 B.C. The story in 2 Kings needs to be read with the awareness that years of telling and retelling the story had heightened the miraculous details of the narrative. The point in sharing these stories in biblical times was to emphasize to child and adult alike the great power and influence of Elijah and his successor, Elisha. Elisha could wield the same miraculous powers that Elijah exercised in his lifetime. The passage describes Elijah's being lifted up into heaven. It does not say that he died, however. This has inspired the thinking of Jews and Christians alike for generations. Elijah was to return as a sign that the age of the Lord had at last dawned. Jews to this day set a place for Elijah at the Passover seder meal, harboring the hope that he will return to usher in the day of the Lord at the great holy festival of Judaism.

The Epistle readings:

For the next four weeks we will be reading The First Letter of Paul to the Corinthians. The 18th chapter of Acts provides us with a brief description of Paul's first visit to the important and thriving city of Corinth. Paul spent about 18 months among the people of the city, which was no small investment of time and energy for the roving missionary apostle. No wonder he had strong feelings when he discovered that after he left Corinth, deep divisions had split the young church. While in the city of Ephesus, Paul wrote a letter back to Corinth. Unfortunately, all but a small piece of that letter is lost. We have a reference to it in 1 Corinthians 5:9 and we may have a fragment of it embedded within 2 Corinthians. (See 2 Cor. 6:14—7:1). Paul's letter elicited a response from the Corinthians. They wrote him back asking a series of questions that Paul responds to in our letter under study. (See 1 Cor. 7:1). First Corinthians was probably written in 55 or 56.

As we begin our reading on Monday, it quickly becomes obvious why Paul wrote his letter. Though the great gift of faith in Christ has come to the Corinthian church, Paul has heard of their divisions. There are actually four churches, it would seem. Some call themselves Paul's people, others are Apollos' people, some belong to Cephas (another name for St. Peter) and some to Chloe. How painful those divisions must be to Paul as he writes from so far away.

The Gospel that Paul has proclaimed in Corinth appealed mostly to the lower classes. The wealthy and powerful are caught up in their own wisdom, it would seem. They consider the cross of Christ a ridiculous doctrine to espouse. Paul writes of the folly of the cross as it confronts the wisdom of the world. "For the foolishness of God is wiser than men, and the weakness of God is stronger than men." (1 Cor. 1:25). Perhaps Paul sees the working people who respond to the Gospel as symbols of the weak confronting the false wisdom of the wealthy and powerful.

The Corinthian church received the Spirit of God and not the spirit of the world, we are reminded in Wednesday's text. It is God's Spirit that explores for us the very depths of God's nature. Thus, what the Corinthians have discovered about God is not something they have gained on their own. Rather, it is a gift given through the Spirit. How can they have pride when they should have only praise and gratitude?

Jesus had spoken about raising up a new temple after three days, a temple that was to be his Body rather than a building in Jerusalem. (John 2:19). The people of Corinth are reminded by Paul that they are a part of that temple. Christ must be the only foundation of that building. The "building materials" each Christian supplies for the construction of the temple will finally be tested, Paul warns. That powerful metaphor leads to a warning: "If any one destroys God's temple, God will destroy him, for God's temple is holy, and that temple you are." (1 Cor. 3:16).

"This is how one should regard us, as servants of Christ and stewards of the mysteries of God" (1 Cor. 4:1). The Holy Spirit has opened the Christians to the mysteries of God's presence and to their pilgrimage toward salvation. The Christian is the steward of the great mystery. From that beautiful metaphor, Paul moves on to a defense of his own ministry among the people. God will judge how Paul exercises his stewardship. No one else, none of those other divisive factions of the church, can make the judgment on Paul. Apollos was one of the leaders of the Corinthian church whom Paul trusted. Paul has planted the seed and Apollos has watered it. Both must be humble in the knowledge that they are merely agents of the Lord's action among the people. May their example of humble stewardship and servanthood be an example for the rest of the church at Corinth.

The Gospel readings:

Just as the first Israel moved through the waters of the Sea of Reeds (or Red Sea) into a time of testing and temptation, so Jesus, the new Israel, moves out of his experience in the waters of his baptism immediately into the wilderness of his trial and temptation. Unlike the first Israel, Jesus does not succumb to the temptations. No golden calf here! Realize that the picture given of the temptations is poetic imagery and not literal reporting of the event. Jesus is tempted to follow his own will rather than that of the Father, even at the end of his life. ("Remove this cup from me. . ." Mark 14:36a.) Thus we can look at Monday's reading as a poetic statement of Jesus' struggle to follow perfectly the will of God. Where others before him have fallen, Jesus remains at one with God. The point of the story is not to be lost on the church, the Body of Christ in the world today. Jesus' temptations are ours. The temptations, as Henri Nouwen has said, are to be relevant, spectacular and powerful.* That is the seductive siren call that tempts the church time and again. The powers of the present age will acknowledge our relevance and our spectacular power if we who are the church will just give our subservience to them, rather than to the risen Christ.

---

*Henri Nouwen, *Lectures on Ministry and Spiritual Formation* (New Haven, CT.: Paul Vieth Christian Education Service, Yale Divinity), "Temptation," cassett tape #2.

Week of the Sunday closest to September 21

The Old Testament readings:

Until Wednesday we will be reading legendary accounts of Elisha's life among the people of the northern kingdom of Israel. They are stories that grew up around the great prophet much as stories grew up around some of the great Christian saints of history. Parts of the narrative may have historical bearing, but most are the kinds of stories parents tell children in each generation to express the awe that is felt toward great figures in history. They are delightful stories, on the whole. They show us insights into the values and feelings of the people better than any straight historical narrative or theoretical monograph would do.

Why are they so important for us today? They are the stories of our people. To understand our people we must understand and appreciate their stories. Moreover, these would have been the stories that Jesus grew up with. To understand the mind of Jesus, one must walk with Jesus in his own background.

Notice in Monday's reading that the Aramaean healed of his leprosy wanted to take some of Israel's earth back to his own country. Since this God who had cured him was the God of Israel, he would need some of the real estate of the land in order to worship this powerful deity!

In the revelation that Elijah experienced on Mt. Horeb, he heard in his mind the command of the Lord to anoint Jehu king of Israel. On Thursday and Friday we see that command carried out by Elijah's successor, Elisha. Jehoram is Ahab's and Jezebel's son. Elisha instigates a coup to unseat Jehoram in favor of Jehu. The evil influence of Ahab and Jezebel has to be eliminated from the social fabric of Israel.

The times are politically dangerous. The prophet sent to do the anointing must flee moments after he pours the oil on the head of Jehu. Notice the importance that the act of anointing has in immediately signifying kingship in the name of God. It is God's prophet who does the anointing, and the act becomes an "outward and visible sign" that God has chosen Jehu for rule. Jehu's companions immediately proclaim him king.

Jezebel dresses for her death, knowing that she will be killed on the arrival of the new king. Her deliberate insult only hastens her awful end. The details of her death may be more than you want to know, but the author of the narrative wanted to drive home the point that what had been foretold by a prophet would be carried out in due time. Prophets were listened to! Jehu's family dynasty lasted from 842 to 745 B.C. He worked to re-establish the just demands of the covenant.

On Saturday you will need to switch your citizenship to the southern kingdom of Judah. It is the year 841 B.C. The mother of King Ahaziah is the daughter of Ahab and Jezebel. Not the best credentials for the royal family of Judah! When her son, Ahaziah, is killed in battle she sees her chance to take power. Jehoida, the high priest of the Temple in Jerusalem, engineers a coup against the queen mother. Prophets and high priests were intimately involved in the political affairs of the state because the state was seen as the realm of Yahweh.

The Epistle readings:

Our reading in 1 Corinthians this week opens with biting words of sarcasm. The Corinthians seemed to feel superior to the apostle who saved them in Christ! It is as if they have already decided that the reign of God has dawned for them, shutting out the very one who brought them the Good News of salvation. The pain mixed with anger that Paul must have been feeling as he wrote this letter, comes across clearly as we read his words. The apostle proclaims weakness while the Corinthians seem to parade their power. May the Corinthians take Paul and Apollos as their model and live in humbleness and expectancy rather than in pride and competiveness. Paul warns of his impending visit.

On Tuesday we move into the second major section of the letter in which Paul addresses the problems inherent in leading the Christian life in the midst of a fallen society. He responds to the questions the Corinthians have asked him in their letter, and he speaks to situations that have arisen during his absence. For example, he has heard that a man in the church has either married or is living with his stepmother. According to Leviticus, this was strictly prohibited for Jews. Paul makes his judgment out of his study of Torah. The penalty for such an illicit relationship was death, according to Leviticus. Paul condemns the man to excommunication that will lead to his death: ". . .you are to deliver this man to Satan for the destruction of the flesh, that his spirit may be saved in the day of the Lord Jesus." (1 Cor. 5:5).

This is an interesting statement of theology as well as a frightening judgment. The man's death was to end in salvation at the day of the Lord. The evils inherent in the man's body would be destroyed, allowing the spirit of the man to find salvation in the Lord. Paul's strict words of condemnation need to be read in the light of the whole Gospel of Christ, a Gospel of mercy and forgiveness—a Gospel that speaks of one's whole being, that is body *and* spirit, made one in Christ; a Gospel Paul himself reflects later in this very letter.

"Christ our Passover is sacrificed for us; therefore let us keep the feast," are words said at the Eucharist during the breaking of the bread. (BCP, p. 364). The origin of those words is the fifth chapter of Corinthians, read on Tuesday.

Evil doers are to be driven from the congregation of faithful. Our mid-week text led to the practice of "shunning" among some Christian bodies over the years. Canon law and prayer book rubrics dealing with excommunication stem in part from Paul's strong directives for the church in Corinth. (BCP, p. 409). Paul was shocked to hear that Christians were dragging each other into pagan courts for judgment. Surely the faithful, who would themselves act as judges even of the angels at the day of the Lord, should be able to judge simple matters of ethics among themselves!

"Do you not know that your body is a temple of the Holy Spirit within you, which you have from God? You are not 'your own,' you were bought with a price. So glorify God in your body." (1 Cor. 6:19-20). We are not free to do anything, as some of the Corinthians were obviously saying. We are only free to act for Christ in the world. Earlier in this letter, we learned that the whole church is the new temple of the Lord in the world. Here we are reminded that each individual Christian is to be a temple of the Lord.

Paul's life as a celibate is to be preferred for Christ would return soon. The Christian must live for that imminent coming and not be tied to the relationships and attachments of this world. Don't worry about your status, whether free person or slave, for we are all one in Christ.

Divorce must be avoided at all costs. Paul's rules reflecting both statements attributed to Jesus as well as his own judgments, were set forth for the church living in expectation of Christ's immediate return. Later, the church would modify Paul's ethic as it became evident that the Christian must live for the long haul in the present order.

Notice that one Christian in the family brought salvation to the entire family. It is out of this understanding that infant baptism became a practice in the church. It is the parent's faith that makes the child eligible for baptism.

The Gospel readings:

This week we discover what Jesus meant about coming to fulfill the Law. The 613 commandments of the Torah set forth for the faithful Jews guidelines for every aspect of their lives. The ultimate purpose of life for the Jew was to know and to follow Torah. The commandments were not great burdens to the Jew. They were constant reminders to the faithful of their covenant with the Lord who guided every waking and sleeping moment.

But the commandments of the Law, Jesus would say, were only the top layer of righteousness. One had to go to the heart of the intent of the Torah commandments to truly respond to God's covenant. For example, anger is the seedbed for murder. Even to feel anger for another means that one has stepped outside of God's intention for man and woman. Loving one's neighbor, as Torah commands, is only the beginning of what it means to love. We must learn to love our enemy, as well as our neighbor. Jesus' words on the Law speak of a new ethic.

This ethic of the kingdom of heaven makes little sense in terms of the ethic of the present age, but God calls us to live as if the kingdom has already fully come. The church is the forerunner of the kingdom. The church must provide glimpses of what that kingdom will be.

Notice the admonition in Matthew 5:23-24, that we must make peace before going to the altar. We are called in the liturgy of the Holy Eucharist to pass the peace, either at the offertory or right before the administration of the sacrament. The peace is not just a simple greeting between people. It is a vivid reminder of Jesus' words.

The restrictions on divorce that Jesus promulgated need to be read in the light of divorce customs of the time. Under some rabinic interpretations, a man could divorce his wife with a mere statement of intent. The wife had few protections. Jesus' words gave women some rights. Marriage was not to be taken lightly.

Thursday's admonition on prayer was not meant to denounce all forms of public worship. Humility is the key to prayer. One must avoid acts of officious public piety. The Lord's Prayer is the model prayer for Christians. Note well the petitions that can lose their impact through familiarity. We pray that the kingdom may come "on earth as it is in heaven." It is the ethic of the kingdom, not the ethic of the world that demands our allegiance. We pray for the bread that will sustain us. We have no right for a wealth of bread, only that which we need for the daily life. Then comes the petition of radical forgiveness. To paraphrase: Forgive us to the extent that we are able to forgive others. In Jewish practice one cannot pray for something one is not willing to do.

The temptation or test is the final trial that comes at the end of the age. We pray that we may be spared the anguish of that period of trial and testing. May we be spared from evil, or the evil one, at that moment and at every moment.

The Lord's Prayer is spoken from heaven in the sense that it prays as God would have us pray, rather than as we would conceive of praying. The Lord sees our need in terms of the need of all humanity. We view prayer from our limited perspective in which we seem to be at the center of the universe. To pray the Lord's Prayer is to see momentarily through the eyes of God.

Week of the Sunday closest to September 28

The Old Testament readings:

Some time has slipped by since we put the Bible down on Saturday. It is now 732 B.C. and we read of the fall of the northern kingdom of Israel to Assyria and the deportation of most of the landed people and their leaders to exile. Picture your mind the tragic march of refugees we've seen in so many periods of history, including our own.

Israel's last king was Hoshea who for a time was willing to be a vassal to the powerful king of Assyria. Unfortunately, he became convinced that an alliance with Egypt would save him from Assyria's domination. The tragic deportation was the result. The rest of Sunday's reading is a theological reflection by the author who wrote a century later. Israel's fall came because the nation had strayed from the covenant.

The hatred for the Samaritans, so evident in the time of Jesus, comes partly out of the feelings we read about on Monday. Settlers from nearby areas were sent into Israel. They brought with them their foreign religious cultic practices. Israel is now an alien and unclean territory for Judah.

We step out of 2 Kings for a day and pick up the narrative in 2 Chronicles, written during the fourth century before Christ. The chronicler wrote a glowing account of Hezekiah's reign in the southern kingdom of Judah, which came right after the fall of Israel (716-687 B.C.) Hezekiah attempted to restore the cultic practices of Yahweh at the Temple in Jerusalem in a way that had not been done in some years. He encouraged the fallen people of Israel to join in a great celebration of the Passover. The numbers of people involved and the animals sacrificed have probably been exaggerated.

Back to 2 Kings for our Wednesday reading. Judah has also fallen to the temptation of relying on Egypt for support against Assyria. We meet Isaiah, the prophet, who is furious with Hezekiah for relying on Egypt rather than Yahweh for protection from Assyria. Now the helpless Hezekiah turns to Isaiah for advice and the prophet tells the king once again that it will be the Lord's might that will save Judah.

Thursday's and Friday's assigned texts make fascinating reading as Sennacherib's agents attempt to demoralize the Jews who sit on the walls of Jerusalem. A terrible plague sweeps through the Assyrian forces. The destruction of the army is understood by the Jews as an act of God.

Saturday we read a taunting song written by Isaiah. God has saved the people for another day. A remnant survives to carry on the covenant with the Lord. 2 Kings 19:29-31 may seem confusing: Isaiah speaks in prophetic form. Judah will not have a full harvest for three years. The first year Judah must eat what grows voluntarily in the field. Food will be short. The second year the only crops will be those that spring from the "volunteer" crops. By the third year Judah shall have a full planting and a full harvest. The land shall be at peace.

The Epistle readings:

With thoughts of Christ's imminent return in mind, Paul urged the Corinthians to remain celibate. One who was married would be distracted from serving Christ. The Christian must be ready to travel light. Paul's words still guide the Roman Catholic Church in her insistence on celibate priests and members of religious orders.

The superior attitude of some Christians in the Corinthian Church was Paul's next concern in his letter. Recent converts to Christ and some of the brothers and sisters who still felt bound by dietary restrictions of the Torah, refrained from eating meat purchased in the market place because it may have been sacrificed to a pagan god. Paul's words to the church were clear. Though the eating of meat could not destroy one's relationship to Christ, if the conscience of other Christians was offended by the practice, then the meat must not be eaten in their presence. The duty of love must outweigh the freedom enjoyed in the Gospel.

Having admonished the Corinthians to curb their freedom so as not to cause offense to the weaker members, Paul reminded them that he had practiced such restraint himself in his life with them. He had freedom to be married and freedom to expect support from them in return for bringing them the Gospel. But Paul would not compromise his witness by putting himself in a position where others might claim that he profited from the Gospel. To the Jews he became like a Jew even though he lived with the knowledge that the ritual code of the Torah was superseded by the freedom of the Gospel. To the gentiles, he spoke like a gentile in order to win them to the Gospel. He lived and breathed as one training for an athletic event. Nothing less would do. No distractions could deter him. His life of total dedication was to be an example for the Corinthians.

Paul spoke to the Corinthians with an authority earned from his seeing the risen Christ on the road to Damascus. (1 Cor. 9:1). Thus, he could speak in the name of Christ and he could speak out of his own personal feelings as an apostle. He carefully made a distinction between the two sources.

For Christians who felt they had already won their salvation through baptism and through participating in the Lord's Supper, Paul had a severe warning. The Israelites, were fed by God in the wilderness just as the Christians were fed by God at the Eucharist, but that did not save them when they succumbed to temptations. As a result, they died never having seen the Promised Land of God. The wilderness became a metaphor in Paul's mind. The Corinthians were to take warning and resist the temptations encountered on their pilgrimage. However, God would not test them beyond what they could bear.

The Gospel readings:

Familiar words greet us as we begin our week in Matthew: "...therefore I tell you, do not be anxious about your life..." (6:25). To be a part of the coming kingdom of heaven means a total concentration on responding to the Lord. "Travel light" is the message. The more things we give ourselves to think about, the less we can be a part of the new order. Alcoholics Anonymous has a saying that guides the lives of its members:

"One day at a time." Take the day, live it fully, and trust that the next day will take care of itself.

The Golden Rule is a part of Tuesday's reading (Matthew 7:1-12). A potpourri of Jesus' sayings was collected by the writer of the gospel, sayings about prayer, forgiveness and Christian attitudes in life. "Do not give dogs what is holy" is a saying Matthew inserted into this section. Perhaps Jesus meant "don't burn yourself out on those who do not respond to the Gospel."

We conclude our reading of the Sermon on Thursday. *Do* the word is Jesus' final admonition, don't just listen to it. We live for the reign of heaven, not for the reign of the present age. We become radicalized in the sense of being forced to go back and look at the very roots of our response and actions as people. The Christian is to be salt and light in society because the Christian is called to live by a different ethic and value structure than the rest of society. Is it any wonder that we are called to confession and penance as a part of our Christian life?

To go into the home of a gentile would make a Jew unclean. Can you imagine the shock of the people as they saw Jesus talking to a Roman centurion? Not only was this man a gentile, he was an officer in the army of occupation!

Friday's reading needs to be read in the light of the customs of Jesus' day. Radical things are happening as this Jesus so casually talks to Jew and gentile alike. The miracle is not restricted to the healing of the centurion's servant. The miracle comes partly in an attitude that seems incomprehensible to the established order.

Matthew 8:11-12 refers to the messianic banquet, the metaphor of the kingdom of God.

We end our week in Matthew with the same note we began on.

There can be no division of commitment. Don't be anxious about the present order for the kingdom of heaven is breaking into history. Family ties are important, but one cannot wait for a father to die and things to be right at home before going off to follow the path of the Lord. Jesus commands the elements, as well as the attention of men and women. Jesus comes as

Savior; one who saves, heals, makes whole again. The prayer of the disciples can be our prayer, too: "Save, Lord; we are perishing." (Matthew 8:25).

Week of the Sunday closest to October 5

The Old Testament readings:

Hezekiah's story continues as we pick up the saga of Judah's difficult years. Poor little Judah sitting at the "hinge" of the Mediterranean world! Sitting between Egypt and Assyria, she was vulnerable to the whims and power dreams of one ruler after another.

We've been reading this great history of Israel and Judah for some weeks. By this time you're familiar with the theological bias of the writers. Nothing is an accident; everything is an "act of God."

In reading Samuel and Kings it often sounds as if God is speaking from the heavens. Always realize that God's words are the interpretations of prophets and historians. As Christians we, too, are called to perceive history through the eyes of the Lord, and sometimes the church is called to speak prophetically in "the name of the Lord." This is the role of the church in society and has been since biblical times.

We get mixed messages about Hezekiah. The writer of Chronicles sings his praises. The writer of Kings is far more reserved. Obviously the prophet, Isaiah, is less than enthusiastic. Judah is a vassal of the Assyrian King. What a sad comedown from the great day of King David and King Solomon.

King Josiah reigned from 640 to 609 B.C. He was the last great king of Judah, and he began a major religious revival when he destroyed all the pagan places of worship. While his workmen were repairing the Temple, they discovered a scroll that seemed to contain a last great sermon of Moses to the Israelites just before Moses' death. This discovery is the present Book of Deuteronomy, the last book of Torah (the first five books of the Old Testament).

Actually, the book was probably written either during the reign of Hezekiah or during the first years of Josiah's reign. Judah needed a vision of hope and a demand for obedience to the one God. Deuteronomy and the deuteronomic history fulfilled this need.

Before reading Thursday's assigned text, flip back to 1 Kings 13 so that you can appreciate how the historian saw Josiah's actions as fulfilling earlier prophecies. An important piece of the story is left out of our assigned reading between Thursday and Friday. Read 2 Kings 23:26-35 for the telling of Josiah's untimely death at the hand of Egypt's Pharaoh. Assyria's empire was crumbling. Egypt was on the move to shore up that empire and grab some land for herself. Josiah went out to oppose that action and lost his life, leaving Judah wide open to disaster. The historian was careful to explain that it was Manasseh's sins that caused the downfall, sins that could not be cancelled in the Lord's mind even by the faithful acts of Josiah.

King Nebuchadnezzar of Babylonia now comes onto the scene. We read again of our biblical ancestors being deported to a foreign land, to live in exile. Picture that tragic scene as you read Friday's assigned text.

We step into the book of the prophet, Jeremiah, on Saturday because he was a contemporary of Josiah's and lived at the time of the deportation. The Rechabites were to Judah what the Amish are to our culture. They lived as their ancestors had lived in the wilderness with Moses. They would do nothing to compromise the kind of response to God that their ancestors had shown before settling in the land of Canaan. Jeremiah contrasted their faith with the decadence of Judah.

The Epistle readings:
This is a heavyweight week in Paul's First Epistle to the Corinthians, for we deal not only with Paul's feelings about the Eucharist, but with his well-known words about spiritual gifts.

Paul has just assured the Corinthians that they did not need to worry about eating meat that might have been sacrificed to pagan gods. As we begin our reading this week, Paul is concerned about Christians who *knowingly* take part in pagan rituals that include eating sacrificial meat. They should know that as they take the cup and share in the bread of the Eucharist they are "sharing in the body of Christ." (1 Cor. 10:16). Consequently, they also realize that knowingly to eat meat sacrificed to a demon is to reject their oneness in Christ and to join themselves to the demon!

In this negative admonition about refraining from pagan sacrificial meals, we also have a positive statement about the Eucharist. To share the cup and bread of Christ is actually to share in the body of Christ. It is to become one with Christ and one with the whole people of Christ, the church. Paul then returns to his earlier concern about accidentally eating meat sacrificed to idols. Eat the meat sold in the market place, Paul says. After all, ". . .the earth is the Lord's and everything in it." (1 Cor. 10:26). Our freedom in Christ must always be tempered by our concerns for the whole community.

On Tuesday we move into the third section of the letter dealing with communal worship. We get some fascinating insight into the life of the Corinthian church and probably of other churches established by Paul as well. The Eucharist was obviously celebrated as a part of a meal. Our church potluck suppers may be closer to the Eucharist as celebrated in Corinth than the formal liturgies we celebrate today. The problem was that the fellowship meals had begun to degenerate into factional free-for-alls in which the wealthier Christians did not share with the poorer members of the church. The cup of the Eucharist was lost in the drinking of many cups of wine. What a shocking scene for Paul to contemplate. He reminds the Corinthians of the sacred nature of their Eucharistic meal by recalling the words Jesus used on the night he was handed over to die. These words, of course, form the heart of our Eucharistic act. Since the gospels were written after Paul's epistles, the words we read this week are our earliest written witness to the Eucharist and to the words Jesus used as he shared cup and bread. Ironically, the words and actions of the Eucharist are preserved for us by Paul because of controversy in the church.

If the bread and cup are eaten in a way that the living presence of Christ is not recognized, then the people take the sacrament to their condemnation. No wonder the church has traditionally preceded the act of Eucharist with confession. The passing of the peace at the Eucharist is another vivid reminder to the Christian that we must live in community with brother and sister before receiving the Body and Blood of Christ. If we are not at peace with those around us then we must ". . . leave your gift there before the altar and go; first be reconciled to your brother and then come and offer your gift." (Matt. 5:24). Thus the passing of the peace is a crucial part of the Eucharistic action of the liturgy. As Paul's words were taken more and more literally over the years, the dreadful nature of the sacrament overshadowed the gift of God's grace revealed in the sacrament. We can see why the Eucharist was received so rarely by Christians in later generations.

"Jesus is Lord" (1 Cor. 12:3) is the earliest recorded Christian creed. It is a statement of absolute faith in Jesus as God. The Apostles' Creed and the Nicene Creed are elaborations of that simple statement of faith. Paul tells the Corinthians that to repeat the creed in faith is to evidence the Spirit in one's life. That is the point Paul makes as he launches into his beautiful words about the unity of life in the Spirit. Each has different gifts but they are all the gifts of the Spirit. The church must live with an understanding that each gift, though different, is essential. If one part of the Body suffers or is rejected, the whole body suffers.

We conclude our week of reading with a dilineation of ministries that were recognized in Paul's churches. Apostles come first, then prophets and so on in descending order. Not everyone is an apostle or prophet, teacher or healer. Not everyone speaks in ecstatic tongues or interprets them. Paul's descending order of ministry would seem to deny the equality of gifts he has just spoken of, but his point is that no one should take pride in a gift. All should aspire for "the higher gifts." That statement leads Paul into the beautiful words from the 13th chapter of 1 Corinthians: "If I speak in the tongues of men and angels, but have not love, I am a noisy gong or a clanging cymbal." (1 Cor. 13:1). Often read out of context, this passage really crowns all that we have been reading this week. We cannot take pride in the gifts that God has given us for ministry. That false pride was the downfall of the Corinthians and is the downfall of each of us. The moment a gift of the Spirit becomes a badge of distinction and a means of judging another person, then the Christian must stand under the judgment of the greater demand of love.

The Gospel readings:

Monday's story is also found in the Gospel of Mark. (See my comments for Thursday, proper 11, year 1 on page 50.) Jesus drives demons out of two men (in Mark it is one man), and the demons go into a herd of pigs. We don't use the language of demons to describe mental or physical disorders today, though we have certainly all experienced the sense of being "out of control" at times. Jesus was and is master over that which alienates us from God, from each other, from wholeness. God has the power to heal us. That is the faith we are called to live out as Christians.

The detail about the demons going into the swine would make a good story for a Jewish audience, since swine were anathema to the Jews. The response of the townspeople is one of fear. "This man's power is too frightening for us to handle. Get him out of here."

Tuesday's story of the paralyzed man is found in the Gospel of Mark; see my comments for Tuesday, proper 10, year 1 on page 46.

Jesus' admonition that new wine cannot be placed in old skins nor new patches be sewn on old clothes concludes our Wednesday reading. These are words that may slide by our consciousness because of their familiarity. The reign of God, the good news of the Gospel, cannot be simply "sewn over" the present system. We cannot adapt ourselves into the old structures where the principalities and powers of the present age hold forth. We must reject the present order and turn to the reign of heaven if we are to know the healing presence of Christ and participate in the reign. The Gospel of Jesus Christ is radical; it calls into question all our assumptions about national purpose, economic justice, personal relationships, values and hopes for the future.

Thursday's and Friday's readings provide us with summaries of all that Jesus did that showed his power to save, even to the point of bringing life to the dead. These are proclamation stories told to convince the unconverted and to strengthen the faith of the church.

Week of the Sunday closest to October 12

The Old Testament readings:

We shift our attention this week from 2 Kings to the Book of Jeremiah. This enables us to pick up some of the intricacies of the historical situation that is explored by Jeremiah in more detail than in 2 Kings.

King Jehoiakim, whose name greets us as we begin our week of reading on Sunday, reigned for 11 years, from 609 to 598 B.C. Babylonia was now the power in the Middle East. King Nebuchadnezzar's armies roamed the area striking terror wherever they went. The once powerful Assyrian armies fell to Babylonia at the battle of Megiddo in 609. Jehoiakim began his reign as a pawn of Egypt, the other power nation on the scene. Sometime in the year 605 B.C. Nebuchadnezzar soundly defeated the Egyptian armies. Jehoiakim quickly transferred his allegiance to the Babylonians, but he could never give up the hope that Egyptian power could somehow neutralize the power of the Babylonians.

Acting directly against the advice of the prophet, Jeremiah, Jehoiakim rebelled against the Babylonians, aligning himself with Egypt. The action brought Nebuchadnezzar and his powerful army to the walls of Jerusalem in the year 598. Jehoiakim died and his sucessor, King Jehoiachin, reigned for three short months. With his surrender to the Babylonians, the elite of the land were taken into exile, leaving behind a weakened remnant that would be unable to rise up in rebellion. Jehoiachin's uncle, Zedekiah, became vassal king of Judah, serving at the behest of the Babylonians, but in 589 he dared to rebel also! Again a king of Judah aligned himself with the Egyptians in the vain hope of throwing off the yoke of the Babylonians.

Again the alliance with Egypt only resulted in the armies of Babylonia returning to the city walls of Jerusalem for a major siege that began in December of 589 B.C. The siege was lifted once when Egypt threatened Babylonian supremacy in the area. Hope was felt again by king and people, but the Egyptian threat was quickly put down and the people found themselves staring out at the vast army of the Babylonians. Finally in 587 B.C. the city walls were taken. Zedekiah stood by and watched helplessly as his sons were killed. His eyes were then put out, and he was marched off in fetters to captivity in a foreign land.

This is the historic situation that prevailed at the time of the writings we read this week. It is assumed that Jeremiah's secretary, Baruch, offered the accounts found in Jeremiah 36:1—45:5, a record of Jeremiah's persecutions at the hand of Judah's kings. Jeremiah was roundly hated by the leaders of the day because he totally opposed the alliances with Egypt.

His message was that the nation must repent and return to the covenant with the Lord. Without repentance, the nation must expect punishment from God. That punishment was conquest and deportation at the hand of the Babylonians. Don't fight the Babylonians and align yourselves with Egypt, Jeremiah insisted, fight your own sinfulness, repent and return to the Lord. When deportations came, Jeremiah expressed his hope for the future as lying with the people being led off into captivity, rather than in any thought that God would sustain the rebellious plans of king and people left behind.

Imagine a prophet of our own time telling us that we should not concentrate on arming ourselves against Communist nations. Our problems, the prophet would say, lay with our own decadence as a nation. If Russians are threatening us, it is because God is sending them to chastise us. Can you imagine the welcome this propeht would receive in the East Wing of the White House, or in the halls of Congress? Now you can understand the setting of Jeremiah's writings!

We return to the book of 2 Kings on Saturday for a few closing summary statements about the last moments of Judah's life as a nation.

The Epistle readings:

Our reading continues in the First Epistle to the Corinthians. Not only were the Corinthians divided as to whom they considered their leaders, but they must also have been divided as to the question of who had the greater gifts of the Spirit. It would seem that those who spoke in ecstatic speech (glossolalia) were causing the greater problem for the young church.

If love is the first test of whether one is truly sharing the gift of the Spirit, the building up of the Body of Christ is the second test. Words that don't inspire or instruct the faithful are destructive, Paul warns. In 1 Corinthians 14:21, read on Wednesday, Paul quotes the prophet Isaiah as proof that speaking in strange tongues without interpretation is reserved for "unbelievers" or pagans. (Actually, Paul takes Isaiah's words out of context. Isaiah was warning the people of Judah that if they did not listen to God's prophets, they would have to listen to the strange speech of the Assyrians who would invade their land as a sign of God's displeasure.) Paul goes on to lay down restrictions for those who would speak in tongues.

On Friday and Saturday we move into another section of Paul's letter. Here he gives us an outline of the Gospel he has been preaching and teaching to the churches. The opening words of the 15th chapter read like Paul's own personal creed.

Then Paul moves to a defense of his doctrine of the resurrection. Apparently some in the Corinthian church were questioning the fact and power of the resurrection. How could they be saying such a thing, Paul asks incredulously? "But if there is no resurrection of the dead, then Christ has not been raised; if Christ has not been raised, then our preaching is in vain and your faith is in vain." (1 Cor. 15:13-14).

Saturday's lection ends with a strange statement about the practice of persons being baptized for those who have already died. Apparently this was a local practice in Corinth. Paul simply mentions it as another example of the faith people have in resurrection. "Since the mention is so unspecific and there is no information from any other New Testament writing (nor, it may be added, in the apostolic fathers), the practice must be considered a curious anomaly, which apparently dropped out of view until revived by some second-and-third-century sectarians."*

---

*1 Corinthians, by William F. Orr and James A Walther, Anchor Bible, Doubleday and Co., p. 337.

The Gospel readings:

We began reading the second major teaching section of the Gospel of Matthew last Saturday. The 12 disciples were named, and we learned that Jesus instructed them. This week we read those instructions. In a fashion similar to the way Matthew strung together familiar sayings of Jesus into a "Sermon on the Mount," Matthew also collected sayings in this section appropriate to the training of the disciples. The Gospel of Matthew was written partly as a manual of instruction for the young church.

Jesus saw his personal ministry as being limited to the Jews. His first instruction to the disciples about going only to the lost sheep of Israel was countered in his final commissioning to the disciples at the time of the resurrection. (See Matthew 28:19).

Travel light and don't waste time with people who are not open to the new reign that is coming. Don't tie yourself down with a lot of possessions and problems that will keep you from proclaiming the reign of God in word and act. These are the warnings Jesus gave his disciples and the primitive church.

Persecution is guaranteed for the disciple of Christ, Jesus warned. The reign of God comes into inevitable conflict with the standards of the present age, and people will resist, Jesus warned. His words about the imminence of the coming of the Son of Man may seem confusing as we look back at Jesus through nearly 2,000 years of history. Jesus warned his followers to live with the constant expectation that the end of the age and the Lord's day of judgment were imminent.

In 70 A.D. Jerusalem and the Temple were destroyed. This terrible moment in history for Jesus' people was, indeed, a day of judgment. If not *the* day of judgment, it was certainly a forerunner of it. In our own time we can see events that point to final judgment, crisis times when we stand under judgment as a person, as a nation and as a society.

Thursday's words are harsh. Jesus did not come to bring peace, but the sword. That is the experience of the church, of Christian martyrs, prophets and activists throughout history. Think of the Christians of Poland, the Martin Luther Kings, the men and women who have stood for the Gospel against oppression and injustices, the Christians persecuted in Central America. There can be no compromise with evil, even when it means standing against one's family.

On Friday we conclude the teaching section to the disciples and begin a new section of Matthew's Gospel, one dealing with increasing controversy with the Jews, along with a series of Jesus' parables. Words about John the Baptist open this section. The least of those who have accepted Jesus are greater than John because they have personally experienced the breaking in of the reign of God. John was only the announcer of this day.

Week of the Sunday closest to October 19

The Old Testament readings:

This week a lot of history is covered. We begin where we left off. Jeremiah's letter to he exiles in Babylonia picks up the story for us on Sunday. "Settle down, support the people you are living with, marry, raise families and make the best of things. You are going to be in this land for a long time. Don't get your hopes up about any rebellions back home that will end this exile." That is Jeremiah's message to the exiles. But notice the words of encouragement included with the admonitions to settle down:

> You will seek me and find me; when you seek me with all your heart. I will be found by you, says the Lord, and I will restore your fortunes and gather you from all the nations and all the places where I have driven you, says the Lord, and I will bring you back to the place from which I sent you into exile. (Jeremiah 29:13-14).

Contrast these words of hope with Psalm 137, written by one who was living in Babylonian exile: "How shall we sing the Lord's song in a foreign land?" (Verse 4). Jeremiah makes a shocking statement. You *can* sing the Lord's song. You *can* pray to the Lord and you can know the Lord wherever you are. God is not tied to a piece of land called Judah, nor to a Temple in Jerusalem.

Jeremiah was forcibly taken to Egypt by a group of Jews. Monday's reading gives us an idea of the disdain he had for those who went to Egypt hoping that they could find a strong enough base of opposition with Egyptian help to overthrow the Babylonian influence on their homeland.

On Tuesday and Wednesday we move to another book of the Old Testament, Lamentations. This book was written during the deportations and the destruction of Jerusalem. Our first selection reflects the deportations in 597, while the second selection raises a lament over the destruction of the city and Temple in 587 B.C. Lamentations gives us a first hand account of the feelings associated with the tragic experience of defeat that came to the once proud city of Jerusalem.

Forty-nine years are going to slip by between Wednesday's and Thursday's readings. When you open to the Old Testament reading on Thursday, the year will be 538 B.C. Cyrus of Persia has effectively destroyed the Babylonian empire, and one of his early actions as a victor over the Babylonians is to allow our biblical ancestors to return to their homeland and to reconstruct the Temple. Actually, many of the Jews chose not to return. They had, indeed, made a life for themselves in a foreign place and did not want to risk the uncertainties of a return to an impoverished land.

For this post-exilic story we turn to the book of Ezra, which is part of a longer unit of work that includes 1 and 2 Chronicles, Ezra and Nehemiah. The entire work forms a unit written sometime during the fourth century B.C. The chronicler had a deep interest in the Temple and could have been a Levite or cantor there. The main point of his message is that the Jewish people are called not so much to national prominence as a great political power, but rather a people set apart by the strict practice of their religious rites, cultic practices and following the Law as laid down by Moses. The Jews are called to become what we would describe as a church.

The books of Ezra and Nehemiah pick up the story after the return from exile. In fact, however, the entire work is a theological treatise more than a history. The point of Chronicles, Ezra and Nehemiah is to trace the cultic life of the people.

The Epistle readings:

Paul's beautiful words about the resurrection remain our focus for the first three days of this week as we continue our reading in 1 Corinthians 15. Portions of this chapter are suggested for reading at the Burial of the Dead along with Isaiah 25:6-9, the origin of part of Paul's quotation in 1 Cor. 15:55. (BCP, pp. 494-95).

On Thursday we hear of Paul's collection for the church in

Jerusalem. Paul tells us in the second chapter of Galatians why he felt so determined to raise money for the poor in the church in Jerusalem. James, Peter and John—apostles active in the Jerusalem church—accepted Paul and Barnabas as partners in the spreading of the Gospel, but the apostles asked Paul to keep the poor of Jerusalem in mind as he traveled about the Mediterranean. Notice the call for the collection on the "first day of the week." (1 Cor. 16:2). The practice of gathering on Sunday, rather than on the Sabbath (Saturday) was obviously an established custom by the time this letter was written.

On Saturday we read The Letter of Paul to Philemon, a personal note to a leader in the church at Colossae. It would appear that Paul was writing from Rome where he was kept under house arrest. Philemon's slave, Onesimus, had run away, but had become a close companion of Paul's during his imprisonment. Paul asks Philemon to welcome his slave back, foregoing the usual punishment for runaways. Paul hints that he would like to have Onesimus back himself, for the slave had become a comfort to Paul during the time they had been together. The letter is delightful to read. Notice the not-so-subtle pressure Paul puts on this Christian leader. A little pious arm-twisting seems appropriate to Paul as he supports his friend, Onesimus. Colossians 4:4-7 contains a reference to Onesimus' return to Colossae, incidentally.

The Gospel readings:

Strong words of condemnation spoken by Jesus are heard this week. He is beginning to run into the blindness and disbelief of his own people. The feelings of frustration and anger are evident in Jesus' response to the people who surround him with such disbelief and open opposition. Even the people of Sodom would have responded more than the people of the towns Jesus has been visiting!

In the Jews' attempt to discover Wisdom by intricate study and practice of the Torah, they have made themselves blind to the possibility of the new covenant in their very midst. "You can't see the trees for the forest," Jesus might have said. Jesus' yoke is far lighter than the yoke of the Torah that the Jews took on so willingly. The simple and uneducated could respond to Jesus. They are far humbler because they know that their righteousness can never be earned by study or ritual practice.

Sabbath practices are the issue in Wednesday's reading. In the strict keeping of the Torah nothing that even vaguely resembles work can be done. And yet, Jesus quickly points out, the Temple priests themselves "worked" in the act of carrying out their duties. King David, when he first escaped from King Saul, used sacred bread for the profane act of surviving. (1 Samuel 21:1-9). Surely Sabbath and ritual laws should not be followed to the point where they take precedence over compassion and healing.

Thursday's reading (Matthew 12:15-21) may not be clear. Jesus quotes from one of the Suffering Servant Songs found in the second part of the book of Isaiah. Those poems describe one who is to come whose suffering for justice will bring redemption and healing to all the people. The suffering servant referred to in the poems could have been a collective reference to the role of the Jewish people in history, but Christians quickly identified Jesus as that suffering servant and Jesus makes that identification himself in this text.

The reference on Friday to the unforgiveable sin of slander against the Holy Spirit may come as a surprising statement in light of Jesus' many words of forgiveness and grace. One way of interpreting Jesus' enigmatic statement is to realize that if a person attributes the gifts of the Holy Spirit to the devil or fails to recognize the gifts at all, then that person cannot be open to the possibility of God's forgiveness in this age or in the age to come.

Jesus' frustrations with his own generation are felt again on Saturday. The Queen of Sheba (or Queen of the South) had sense enough to journey to Jerusalem to hear the wisdom of God's chosen king, Solomon. The people of Ninevah had wisdom enough to repent and thus escape destruction. They didn't waste time asking Jonah for a sign. They acted when they heard his word of warning. The present generation is so wicked and blind that they demand a sign before they will believe.

Week of the Sunday closest to October 26

The Old Testament readings:

The prophets, Haggai and Zechariah, lived at the time of the restoration of Jerusalem and the Temple, and their writings are included at this point in our historic survey.

Haggai was disturbed that the returning exiles were not immediately working to rebuild the Temple. The draught and general malaise of the people were signs of God's wrath directed against the people for not building the Lord a house while they lived in their own houses, he pointed out.

Zechariah wrote in the visionary language that characterized the late Old Testament writings. His role was to encourage the people. They had suffered long enough for the sins of their ancestors. God would restore them, he promised. The rebuilding of the temple would be a sign that God's wrath was ended and a period of restoration as God's people had begun.

Both Haggai and Zechariah wrote in the second year of King Darius of Persia, 520 B.C. When Zerubabel, a descendant of King David, was appointed by Darius to be governor of the region, hopes were raised that he would restore the throne of David. That hope was never to be realized.

Now that Temple construction is in progress at last, we turn our attention to the city walls of Jerusalem. Nehemiah is the important figure for this construction project. We meet him in his position as an official cupbearer to the Persian king, Artaxerxes, who succeeded Darius and ruled from 465 to 423 B.C. Both Ezra and Nehemiah saw their work as a sacred task ordained by God who wanted his glory revealed in temple and in magnificent city. Nehemiah's work is met with ridicule and open hostility from neighboring peoples. The details of the wall construction that we hear at the end of the week read like an adventure story.

The Second readings:

This week we begin a four-week study of the Revelation to John. Because so much confusion and mystery surround this book, people tend to shy away from it, or they take it as literal prophecy of what is to come. Before we start to read Revelation we need to keep a few things in mind. This is a distinctive type of literature called apocalyptic from the Greek word meaning to reveal or to uncover, as in uncovering a mystery. This unique style of literature, *The Interpreter's Bible Dictionary*** tells us, originated in the Persian religious cults and gradually was taken into Jewish literary tradition during and after the Babylonian exile. Look over the Old Testament books of Daniel and Ezekiel and compare them with the material you are reading in Revelation these weeks for the source of some of the imagery.

Apocalypticism rises out of an oppressed people who see their hopes dashed in the continuing oppression of foreign powers. These powers take on the characteristics of evil. The hope that gives courage to the people is that the power of God will finally defeat the power of evil and restore the faithful to a new kingdom prepared for them.

The coded nature of this style of literature hides the true meaning from the oppressor while giving hope to the oppressed. Revelation was written in about 95, during the reign of the Roman emperor, Domitian, an emperor who ruthlessly persecuted the Christian churches of the empire.

Now begin your reading of the book. Place yourself in the historic period of the book's origin. Then think of oppressed Christians living in the world today.

I'll point up a few of the highlights. On Monday we are "lifted up" with John in his vision of heaven. Notice on Monday and all through this book words familiar to us from liturgy, hymn and Christian art. "'I am the Alpha and the Omega,' says the Lord God." (Rev.1:8). "I am the first and the last, and the living one..." (Rev. 1:17-18).

Before beginning your reading on Tuesday, read Isaiah 6:1-9 for his vision of the throne of God. Some of that imagery certainly formed the vision of John. You may again recognize some familiar phrases used in Christian worship. John may well have

---

*Interpreter's Bible Dictionary, Volume 1, Abingdon Press.

inserted portions of Christian liturgy used in his day into his book so that we have a beautiful collection of early Christian hymns and canticles. Canticles 18 and 19 from Morning Prayer come from our reading assigned this week and may well have been early Christian canticles familiar to the writer of Revelation. The four creatures mentioned in Revelation 4:7 became symbols for the four writers of the gospels.

The risen Christ is the Lamb who is worthy to open the scroll. Wednesday's and Thursday's readings sound like a great enthronement or coronation ritual, with songs of praise to the Lamb. Our experience of the Eucharist gives us an experience in the "throne room" of the Lord. We, too, gather at the table or throne of the Lord to offer words of praise and thanksgiving. The imagery of the Eucharist is the imagery of the heavenly kingdom. Listen to the words that are so familiar to us from the liturgy of the Eucharist:

> Therefore we praise you, joining our voices with Angels and Archangels and with all the company of heaven, who for ever sing this hymn to proclaim the glory of your name. (Book of Common Prayer, p. 362).

Eucharist becomes a foretaste, a preview of our gathering to praise the Lamb of God.

The terrible time of final trial becomes the scene halfway through Thursday's assigned reading. This is the "trial," or "temptation," that we pray to be saved from every time we say the Lord's Prayer. God is a God of justice, thus injustice in the present age must be punished. That is the theological perspective of the writer of Revelation.

In the visionary language of the writer, God was now unleashing the promised justice. He was moving to punish the evil doers of the present age and reward the righteous that belong to the new age even while the present age existed. These were the martyrs or the "church triumphant" whom we meet at the end of Thursday's reading. (Rev. 6:9-11).

On Friday in Revelation 6:12—7:4 and on Saturday in Revelation 7:4-17 the contrast of the rewarding of the righteous is placed in juxtaposition to the trials of the wicked. The 144,000 is a symbolic number meaning all those who have been purified through their struggle in the church of Christ. Persecution and struggle in the present age growing out of their commitment to the Lamb mark their life among the favored. Notice the liturgical phrases that jump out of the text in Revelation 7:10, 12.

The Gospel readings:

We are in the midst of a section of Matthew's Gospel devoted to the controversies Jesus had with the Jewish authorities and with the disbelief of the people with whom he came in contact. If Jesus' words sound harsh, realize the struggle he was undergoing personally. Let us not picture him a dispassionate Son of God with no human feelings and responses. He deeply feels rejection and conflict, but more importantly he sees his own people turn away from the gift of participating in the reign of God that he has come to announce. Monday's words about unclean spirits returning to an empty house are a picturesque way of saying, "You've got to replace the evil with something good. You have to replace hate with love, injustice with justice, or your last situation will be worse than the first." Jesus' words about his family may seem particularly harsh, but the true family of Christ are those who respond to the urgency of the new age.

Parables are short anecdotes told by rabbis to their pupils in order to deepen the students' understanding. The parable on the surface seems to be a simple story about seeds, sons leaving home or unfaithful servants, but the parable always contains a surprise for the hearer. It doesn't come out the way we think it will. Parables are meant to open us to new ways of perceiving truth.

The gospel writers, in the placement and the explanation they gave the parables, shaped the meaning in ways that Jesus himself would not have foreseen. The readings for Tuesday, Wednesday and Thursday provide a perfect example of this process.

The Parable of the Sower may have been told by Jesus as a way of saying to his disciples, "Don't worry! You need not be discouraged that so many of our people are not responding to the Gospel. Some seed is going to land in the right places, and for that we can rejoice." The writer of the gospel, probably influenced by the needs of the church, turned the parable into an allegory in which each facet of the story stood for something else.

Moreover, Matthew saw the parables as means of conveying secret teaching. "Of course many people turned away from Jesus. He spoke in coded language that was available only to the chosen few," Matthew was saying. This interpretation of Jesus' use of parables helped the church understand the lack of acceptance of the Gospel by so many people.

The Parable of the Weeds, read on Friday, may be another story altered somewhat by the church. A concern in the gospel writer's time was that there seemed to be people in the church who were not living out the Gospel in their lives. An allegorical explanation of this parable will be read on Monday. The allegory expands the focus of the parable to include the judgment rendered all people at the end of time. Saturday's parables—the Parable of the Mustard Seed and the Leaven—remind us that God's kingdom may seem imperceptible at the present moment. It's like a tiny seed, a bit of yeast, but the seed and the yeast grow to unbelievable size.

Week of the Sunday closest to November 2

The Old Testament readings:

Nehemiah was appointed governor by the Persian king, which gave him authority as he worked to strengthen the defenses of Jerusalem and to demand that the Torah be followed faithfully by Jews who had returned from exile. Those were difficult days for the returnees. For some, life had been better in exile than the life experienced back in a desolate homeland. When the leading people of Judah were sent off into exile, the Samaritans gained control of the area. Had Nehemiah and Ezra not taken strong leadership at this particular point in history, four and a half centuries before the time of Jesus, Judaism might not have survived.

Our week with the returned exiles opens with Nehemiah confronting the wealthier citizens. The poorer people are rapidly becoming so deeply in debt, just from the struggle to survive, that they are actually having to put their sons and daughters into enforced servitude to support continuing loans. Nehemiah is forced to take direct action to relieve the poor of the land. He reminds the people that social justice and compassion are at the very heart of the Torah.

You will meet Sanballat, Geshem and Tobiah as the reading opens on Monday. Let me introduce you. Sanballat has official status in the Persian hierarchy as governor of Samaria. Until the return of the exiles, the territory that Nehemiah is now administering has been part of Sanballat's area of authority. Geshem and Tobiah are foreigners living in the area. The three of them plot to both undermine Nehemiah's authority with the Persians and to get him away from the city to kill him. When that attempt fails, they try to convince him, through a well-known and trusted Jew, that his safety lies in entering the Temple for sanctuary. To do so would violate Temple cultic code. We feel the shock of betrayal as Nehemiah realizes that this trusted Jew is in on the plot to discredit him.

Nehemiah works to restore the cultic practices of the Temple as well as to restore the city walls. He is concerned that the cantors, Levites, door keepers and other essential cultic leaders again receive their just portion from the people. His concerns sound not unlike the concerns of the stewardship chairman of the parish church. Keep Nehemiah's concern for the cultic practices of the people in mind as you read Wednesday's text. When he leaves Jerusalem to pay an official visit to Artaxerxes, the people immediately fall away from the prescribed religious practices and on his return Nehemiah finds the Temple deserted. The pledges apportioned for the Levites have not been paid, resulting in the Levites having to return home in order to survive. What is worse, the foreigner, Tobiah, has been allowed to profane the holy storeroom by stashing his personal belongings there! The storeroom is empty because people have not been bringing their portion of food and provisions for the Levites.

On Thursday, we return to the book of Ezra and pick up his story. He returns to Jerusalem later than Nehemiah. He is a "Jewish affairs officer" in the court of Artaxerxes. With talent for persuasion, he convinces the king that promoting Jewish cultic practices in the Jerusalem region will be a tremendous boon to building relations with this subject people out there on the fringes of the kingdom. He, Ezra, is the natural one to send to Jerusalem to make sure the job is done properly. The king responds generously to Ezra's suggestion. Notice the king's understanding that God rules over a particular nation or territory: ". . .the God of Israel, whose dwelling is in Jerusalem. . ." (Ezra 7:15). Little does he realize that the God of Judah claims the whole created order! With the king's commission in hand and with a vast store of treasure to back up the commission, Ezra sets out on his journey to Jerusalem. He does not dare ask for guards since he has boasted that the God of Israel will protect the people on their journey!

We leave Ezra at the end of the week as he expresses horror at the discovery that Jewish men have entered into marriage with non-Jews, against the commandments of the Lord. Prohibitions against intermarriage are found in Deuteronomy 7:3-4. Joshua repeated the prohibition in his final address to the

Israelites before his death. (Joshua 23:12-13).

The Second readings:

Our second readings this week may be heavy going at times, but look behind the symbolism for a suffering, persecuted people seeking signs of hope that God's kingdom is coming. There is no need to try to pin down the meaning of the rather bizarre symbols in the book. Many people have turned to Revelation to forecast the end of the world and the second coming of Christ, but remember the nature of the literature we are reading.

At the same time appreciate the mystery of the writing. Part of the important message of apocalypticism for all of us is that God's powers are not limited to what we can understand and control.

The overall message of Revelation is as relevant for us today as it was for the persecuted Christians of the first century. God, not man and woman, is in control of creation and history, ultimately. We can say this even as we face the possibility of nuclear holocaust. For those who would destroy creation in nuclear war, Revelation must be read as God's judgment. For those who live under the shadow of that destructive power, Revelation provides a hopeful statement that God's creation cannot finally be destroyed.

Friday's reading includes a Christian hymn that is included as Canticle 19 in Morning Prayer. (BCP p. 94). Canticle 18 for Morning Prayer is also taken from Revelation. The several hymns included within this book may be an indication that the heavenly scenes of praise and worship reflect early Christian worship practices including fragments of ancient rites and hymns.

In reading Revelation, remember that one of the characteristics of apocalyptic literature is the writing about the present moment as though it were a historical event. Thus, read "Babylon" as "Rome" on Saturday, and the beasts who will fall to destruction as the Roman emperors and the powers of Rome.

The Gospel readings:

Tuesday's reading (Matthew 13:44-52) emphasizes the need to completely reorient one's life toward the kingdom of God. All Jesus' rather harsh sayings about leaving mother and father behind are expressed in the parables of the treasure found in the field and the merchant finding a fine pearl. Both lucky persons sell everything they have to enjoy the new-found treasure, and so it must be with us as we respond to the Gospel. Our lives must be totally reoriented around the Gospel; this is true conversion. The closing words are rather subtle in meaning. The scribe or teacher of the Law who knows and loves the Torah *and* has discovered the reign of heaven has the distinct advantage of both the old and the new teaching. Such a statement would fit well with a Jewish Christian audience!

With Thursday's reading (Matthew 14:1-12), we begin a new section of Matthew's Gospel. Jesus prepares the disciples for their leadership in the church. We'll be in this major teaching section for the next two weeks as we read through the end of chapter 17.

The death of John the Baptist colors our reading on Thursday with a grim and foreboding feeling. John died in witnessing for God in the face of evil.

The familiar story of the feeding of the 5,000 is the appointed lesson for Friday. The feeding incident on the hillside can be seen as a foretaste of the messianic banquet, just as the Eucharist is a foretaste of our life to come at God's table.

On Saturday we read of Jesus walking on the waters of the lake. He is about to pass the disciples by when he notices their fear. Jesus exercises power over the elements by calming the storm. He walks over the waters that represented death and chaos to ancient peoples. Some scholars feel that this event may have actually been a resurrection appearance, but the power of the story in the early church lay in the hope that the event held out to a church living in confusion, persecution and fear.

Week of the Sunday closest to November 9

The Old Testament readings:

Sunday's reading reveals a painful scene. Jewish men are ordered by Ezra to leave their gentile wives, which meant a splitting up of families. Ezra sees the practice of intermarriage as eventually destroying Judaism. Traditions kept by the family are essential to the maintenance of Jewish life. Intermarriage threatens the carrying out of tradition. This same concern has guided more recent thinking on intermariage between Jews and Christians, between Protestants and Roman Catholics, and still remains an issue for some people today.

We shift from the Book of Ezra to the Book of Nehemiah on Monday in order to pick up the sequence of events as they occurred historically. On Monday we hear of the ritual act that separates Jews from their gentile spouses: "And the Israelites separated themselves from all foreigners, and stood and confessed their sins and the iniquities of their fathers." (Neh. 9:2).

Read the optional portion assigned for Monday (verses 16-25). Beginning in the middle of Nehemiah 9:5 and extending through the text assigned for Tuesday, we read a psalm of praise apparently recited by the people at the moment of separation.

Wednesday's reading moves us back a chapter in the Book of Nehemiah, but scholars feel the event probably followed the separation rite read on Tuesday. The people, now "cleansed' from foreign influence among them, gather to hear the Torah read. Read carefully the ritual that was followed in connection with the reading of the Torah. Ezra and the other leaders stand on a platform and open the book "in the sight of all the people" (Neh. 8:5). Everyone stands at that point. Ezra says words of blessing to the Lord to which the people respond, "Amen, Amen." Next they prostrate themselves and then remain in their places, probably seated, for the reading of Torah, which takes from early morning until noon.

The tradition associated with the reading of the Gospel in the Episcopal Church is found in this ancient chapter of Nehemiah. Today we stand for the reading of the "Law," the

Gospel of Jesus Christ. The reader blesses the Lord, we respond, and then we listen to the Word of God. That Word is then expounded in the sermon. We respond again with the reciting of the Nicene Creed, a statement of faith that the salvation story is true for us. "We believe" in that proclaimed Word and in that living Lord who is revealed in the Word.

The reading of Torah described in Nehemiah 8 is followed by a great celebration in which sweet wine is shared. The "sweet wine" of our celebration could be considered the Holy Eucharist shared in joy. Notice the command to send portions to those who have nothing. Always compassion and concern for the poor lie at the heart of every command.

Thursday we move forward in history to about 165 years before Christ. 1 Maccabees is a book from the Apocrypha that describes the history of this time. The Greeks dominate the area, having replaced the Persians as the political power. The concern of the Greeks is to assimilate all cultures into the Greek idea of life. Jewish tradition is particularly heinous to the Greek mind so severe persecutions of the Jews who refuse to give up their own separated life begins. The "abomination of desolation" referred to in Friday's reading is an altar to a Greek god set up in the Temple in Jerusalem. Saturday's reading introduces Mattathias and his sons who finally take a stand against the Greeks, thus beginning a brutal guerrilla war that eventually drives the Greeks out of Judah.

The Second readings:

Taken as a whole, Revelation is an important book that crowns and completes the Biblical story. Though we may not suffer under persecution now, each of us needs to remember daily that God is ultimately triumphant in history. We are chosen as God's people, empowered with God's spirit, and given a vision of life that surpasses human understanding.

Monday through Wednesday we read the vivid description of total destruction by God's forces of the evil Babylon. Babylon is a code name for Rome. It is Rome that God is going to destroy and punish for her persecution of the Christians.

The fall of Rome is met with awe and terror by the peoples of the world, but with praise and joy by the heavenly throng who see justification done for Rome's sins. Thursday's joy in heaven is matched for the rest of the week by grim scenes of final judgment that shall be visited upon earth. Heaven opens wide once more and a rider on a white horse goes out leading an army of other white-horsed riders. The rider's name is Word of God, a title for Christ. He rides forth in judgment. Note the reference to treading "the wine press of the fury of the wrath of God the Almighty." (Rev. 19:15). Think of this passage and its meaning the next time you sing "The Battle Hymn of the Republic."

We skip over the rather lurid details of the last battle and continue our reading on Saturday in chapter 20. Satan, defeated in the battle with Christ, is chained for 1,000 years. The martyrs in heaven who have died in the persecutions of Rome are brought back to life to reign on earth with Christ for the millennium.

The Gospel readings:

As I mentioned last week, Matthew followed the Gospel of Mark almost word for word in this section. Matthew was spreading the Gospel of Jesus Christ to another area of the church. It was natural that he would use material that he had available from the work of another evangelist.

The writer of the Gospel of Luke also made use of portions of the Gospel of Mark, although both Matthew and Luke adapted Mark's words to fit their unique perspectives and understandings of the Gospel. Because of the similarity between Matthew and Mark in this part of our reading, I refer you to that portion of Mark that we read last summer. As you begin this week in the Gospel, turn back to the notes beginning on Thursday of the week of proper 12, year 1 on page 55 and read through Wednesday of the week of proper 13, year 1.

Friday's reading, however, offers a distinctly different treatment of the same material. I'd suggest that you take a little additional time on Friday to read Mark 8:27-33, then the assigned text of Matthew 16:13-20. What is unique to the Gospel of Matthew is the clear authority given to Peter, who is to be the "rock" upon which Jesus would build his church. This is the scriptural authority for the church to act for Christ from one generation to the next. What the church decides on earth is ratified by God. The church acts, in other words, with the authority of God. This passage may explain the position given to the Gospel of Matthew in the New Testament.

The Episcopal, Roman Catholic and Orthodox churches, moreover, see this passage as establishing the authority of leadership exercised by the bishops of the church. The apostolic authority of Peter has been handed down with the laying on of hands from one generation of bishops to the next. The bishop of the church points directly to the authority to "bind and to loose" granted to Peter.

The name, Peter, incidentally, means "rock." Jesus was making a pun as he gave Simon the added name of Peter. But the one called "rock" soon earned himself the dreaded name of Satan. Peter could not accept the idea that Jesus must suffer and that his followers must suffer as well. Jesus' temptation to follow evil did not end in his wilderness experience. Now temptation came from his closest disciple. Jesus' calling each disciple to take up the cross contradicts the expectations we may have been raised with, too. These words of Jesus confront our values and visions of life just as they confronted Peter's.

Jesus' promise that the Son of Man would come before the present generation passed away can be seen either as an unfulfilled expectation of Jesus or as one that was at least in part fulfilled with the resurrection and the coming of the Holy Spirit to the disciples.

Week of the Sunday closest to November 16

The Old Testament readings:

This week's selections from 1 Maccabees reads like an adventure story. Mattathias and his sons inspire a large group of faithful Jews to leave their homes and go out into the country to begin what we would call guerrilla warfare. Life for those Jews would have been far easier if they had simply agreed to worship the Greek gods. Unlike recent Jewish persecutions, the Greeks accept the Jewish people so long as they are willing to follow Greek religious practices and renounce their Jewish heritage. The Jews of the Maccabean age are not fleeing for their lives; they are fleeing for their faith in the one God.

When the Jews are attacked on the Sabbath, Torah commandments prohibit response. A terrible massacre results. Practical considerations quickly modify the strict following of Torah traditions. On Sunday we meet the forerunners of the Pharisaic sect so familiar to us from the gospels. The Hasideans (meaning pious or faithful) mentioned in 1 Maccabees 2:42 are a set-apart group who attempt to follow the Torah faithfully. We might call them a religious order today. They are the forerunners of both the Essenes and the Pharisees.

Battles are not won by numbers or by mighty armament, we are reminded on Monday. "Victory does not depend on numbers, strength comes from Heaven alone. . . But we are fighting for our lives and our religion." (1 Maccabees 3:19, 21; *New English Bible*). This is a lesson we must remember as a nation today.

The words of Torah take on a kind of oracular significance in the time of the Maccabees, we read on Wednesday (1 Maccabees 3:48). Just as some people open their Bibles and put their finger at random on a verse of scripture to determine God's word for them, so the Jews consult the words of Torah for pointers to God's will. The Nazarites, who are mentioned in Wednesday's reading, are another religious order of the day, and their vows include purification and dedication rites conducted in the Temple. The Temple has been defiled by the

Greeks, making it impossible for the Nazarites to live out their dedication to God.

Notice the litany-like refrain in Thursday's reading: "for it is right, because his mercy endures for ever." (1 Mac. 4:24, *New English Bible*). Praise to the God who brought victory is a natural part of the victory celebration.

We read of the institution of the feast of Hanukkah on Friday. The date the Temple was cleansed and rededicated was December, 164 B.C. The eight-day celebration is symbolized by the nine-branched candelabrum called a menorah, used by present-day Jews to celebrate this festival. (The ninth candle is used to light each of the eight candles on the succeeding days of Hanukkah.) 1 Maccabees 4:54 gives us a picture of the Temple celebration. The prescription for an annual celebration of this feast is clearly set forth in the text. "Do this in remembrance. . ." is a crucial part of Jewish life that carries right into our life in Christ. As festivals that mark past events in the life of Israel are remembered, their power is felt again in the present moment.

We began our great pilgrimage through Israel's history back in the middle of June as we opened 1 Samuel. Saturday's reading from Isaiah places a beautiful doxology to the whole journey we've shared in the church though the daily office these many weeks. The poem from Isaiah describes Jerusalem when the day of the Lord fully dawns in the new age that God will bring about. Long life shall be expected. Suffering shall be ended, and the "wolf and the lamb will lie down together." This perfect reign of peace and justice and total fulfillment is a fitting vision with which to end our journey through history and to look ahead, with the coming of Advent, to the promise of God's perfect reign that began with the birth of Jesus.

The Second readings:

Our reading of Revelation is good preparation for the coming of Advent in two weeks. During Advent we focus on our expectations for the final victory of Christ as well as celebrate the first coming of Christ in Bethlehem. This week in Revelation we read the beautiful description of that victory. After a thousand years in captivity, Satan breaks loose for one more try at seducing the nations of the world. A heavenly fire consumes him and the resurrection of all the dead begins. (The first resurrection was restricted to the martyrs who had died for the Gospel. See Rev. 20:4.) The books of judgment are opened and sinners are separated from the saints.

Tuesday's text introduces the final vision of triumphant culmination. The sea, that represented fear and chaos to ancient peoples, dries up. Out of the heavens "I saw the holy city, new Jerusalem, coming down out of the heaven from God, prepared as a bride adorned for her husband." (Rev. 21:2).

God sitting triumphantly in heaven as "the Alpha and the Omega, the beginning and the end [will]. . .wipe away every tear from their eyes, and death shall be no more, neither shall there be mourning nor crying nor pain any more, for the former things have passed away." (Rev. 21:4). This rich description of God's ultimate victory even over death is one of the texts suggested for reading at the burial office.

The purpose of Revelation is stated succinctly by the writer of the book in Friday's reading: "Let the evildoer still do evil, and the filthy still be filthy, and the righteous still do right, and the holy still be holy. Behold, I am coming soon, bringing my recompense, to repay every one for what he has done." (Rev. 21:11-12).

The Gospel readings:
Refer to Thursday and Friday of proper 13, year 1 for notes on Monday's and Tuesday's readings.

Wednesday's reading includes a strange dialogue between Jesus and Peter about the paying of the Temple tax. Jesus tells Peter that paying the tax is appropriate for the disciples though, as his followers, they are exempt from the obligation. They can pay it out of courtesy, in other words, so as not to offend the Temple authorities. In an offhand remark Jesus directs Peter to look for the coin with which to pay the tax in the mouth of a fish. He might have said, "Go ahead and pay the tax out of respect and to avoid scandal. God provides you with the means of payment with the fish you catch every day."

On Thursday we move into another of Matthew's teaching sections, this one directed to the primitive church. Matthew placed principles of communal life laid down by the church side-by-side with Jesus' sayings remembered by the church, providing a basic guide for church authority and administration.

To enter into the reign of God, we read on Thursday, one must adopt the attitude and nature of a child. This refers to the childlike sense of innocence, but it also requires that we live as children under the authority of the God who comes to us as Father.

Friday's reading lays down clear guidelines for the church in settling disputes among the faithful. Words of authority for this church are set forth in Matthew 18:18-20. Last Friday in Matthew 16:13-20 we read that Peter could act for heaven in binding up and loosing. This Friday we notice that the church is given that same authority. Wherever two or three make decisions, it shall be "...done for them by my Father in heaven." (Matt. 18:19). "For where two or three are gathered in my name, there am I in the midst of them. (Verse 20). Here we see the early church's realization that the Lord was calling them to gather in assembly to seek the guidance of the Lord and to act in his name. These are very early statements of church polity that still govern our life in the church.

Last Friday and this Friday we come across the Greek word, *ekklesia*, which means congregation or church. These are the only times the term is used in the gospels. Matthew's concern for the guidance of this *ekklesia* of Christ is clearly evident all through his gospel, a concern not evident in Mark's gospel which we read this summer. We see an entirely different focus in the two gospels, a reminder that each of us hears the Good News through our experience and our understanding of how God is calling us to live. The Gospel evolves out of the lives of God's people as they interpret the acts of God in their own time. Our week closes with a parable that makes the petition of forgiveness in the Lord's Prayer vivid.

Week of the Sunday closest to November 23

The Old Testament readings:

This week our readings are a selection of writings from the prophets that deal with the coming day of the Lord, that time when God will judge the alien nations and purify and redeem Israel. Advent is the season that looks ahead to that great day. The focus of redemption, however, is no longer just the nation of Israel, but the whole created order. (See Romans 8:18-25). Advent also looks back in history to the dawn of the great day of the Lord, the birth of Jesus the Christ. Thus, Advent is a season of expectancy of God's final triumph in history and creation. These final weeks of the long season after Pentecost move us into the mood of Advent.

The prophet, Joel, is heard on Monday. Joel lived in the time of Nehemiah and Ezra. We are familiar with that historic period, having just read the books of Ezra and Nehemiah. Remember the vindictiveness of that period. Judah retreated within herself and her own traditions as her enemies derided her feeble attempts to regain national and religious stature.

Joel wrote at a time when locusts had swept through the land. He saw in that awesome event the direct hand of God punishing the unfaithful Judah. Our reading takes the plague as a metaphor. The nations who have opposed Judah will be dispersed by God as the locusts were finally dispersed at the end of the plague. The prophet dares the enemies of Judah to arm and come up against the nation. The Lord will take the judgment seat against those nations and destroy them. The people of God will once again be restored. The well-known song, "The Battle Hymn of the Republic," has its roots in Joel 3:13.

On Tuesday we move to the writing of Nahum, the prophet. Our historic setting is Babylonia's rise to power about 612 B.C. Assyria's defeat by Babylonia was a vindication for Judah, the prophet felt. God brought about that Assyrian defeat. God's people would be freed from foreign domination. Nahum did not know what we know from our pilgrimage through the Bible in our daily reading. Babylonia would be the next dominating power on the horizon for Judah, not the hoped-for savior.

Obadiah was a prophet who wrote about 425 B.C., the period of Nehemiah and Ezra. Vindictive statements against Judah's traditional enemy, Edom (Esau, the brother of Jacob, was considered their founding father), is the message of Obadiah. He felt that God would ultimately punish Edom for her acts against Israel and Judah. In the process, Judah's pitifully limited boundaries would be expanded to include all the territories that were held during King David's reign.

So far this week we've read words of ultimate judgment against Judah's enemies. The words reflect the painful feelings of the people as they looked at the devastation of their land. They understood God's judgment as applying to their enemies. Lest we judge too harshly the words of the Old Testament prophets, we need to read the headlines of our own times. Our national leaders assure us that evil lies in the heart of those we perceive as enemies, while righteousness is the property of the United States.

Zephaniah turned the focus of judgment from enemy nations to include judgment of Judah. It will be Jerusalem who will stand condemned at the final judgment for having acted so often against the Word of God. Words of condemnation turn to words of hopeful vision, however, in the last verses of Thursday's reading. People will come from beyond the rivers of Ethiopia; "my suppliants, the daughter of my dispersed ones, shall bring my offering." (3:10). Foreigners will recognize the sovereignty of the Lord and come to worship. Keep this thought in mind during the feast of the Epiphany as we read of "wise men from afar" coming with gifts for the Christ child. The proud and arrogant will be driven out from Jerusalem, leaving "...a people humble and lowly" (3:12) who will respond to God's authority. "Blessed are the poor in spirit, for theirs is the kingdom of heaven," Jesus would say some years later. (Matt. 5:3). He spoke within the context of the words we read on Thursday.

Friday's reading from Isaiah reminds us that there is no escape from he final judgment of God. Feel the power of imagery that unfolds at the prophet's hand.

On Saturday, the last day of the liturgical year, we turn from words of judgment to words of mercy. The concluding portion of Micah, assigned for Saturday, may have been added to the original scroll by a postexilic author who pointed beyond the judgment of God to the tremendous mercy of God.

The Epistle readings:

The First Letter of Peter may have been written by a disciple of Peter, rather than by the apostle himself, since the letter addresses a historic situation of persecution that existed after the apostle's death. A disciple of Peter could have used his teacher's name to add authority to the writing, a common practice of the time. The writing opens in the form of a letter addressed to persecuted Christians living in Asia Minor. Some scholars feel that 1 Peter is actually made up of fragments from an early baptismal liturgy. The writer may have combined the liturgical sections with commentary and admonitions addressed to a church under seige.

Persecution and struggle are the tests of the Christian, we learn from this epistle. Out of the struggle comes a deeper relationship to Christ who continues to suffer for the redemption of the world through the church.

> "In this you rejoice, though now for a little while you may have to suffer various trials, so that the genuineness of your faith, more precious than gold which though perishable is tested by fire, may redound to praise and glory and honor at the revelation of Jesus Christ." (1 Peter 1:6-7).

Verses 1 through 9, read on Monday, may be an early hymn sung at baptisms on Easter morning.

One of the accusations made against Jesus as he stood before Caiphas was that he had been heard to say that he had the power to destroy the Temple and build it up in three days. (Matt. 26:61). Wednesday's text may reflect those words attributed to Jesus. The new Temple is to be the Christians gathered as the church. The cornerstone of the new Temple will be the risen Christ, a cornerstone that many will trip and fall over because they refuse to believe in Christ. For those who do believe, however, the cornerstone becomes their way to be part of a royal priesthood, a chosen people. Psalm 118:22 provided the basis for the writer's thinking, as well as words attributed to Jesus: "The stone which the builders rejected has become the chief cornerstone." The psalmist may have had Israel or one of Israel's kings in mind as he wrote that verse.

A nation rejected by other peoples was the nation favored by God and the chief cornerstone of God's activity in the world. The church quickly applied this metaphor to the risen Christ. Wednesday's lection also mentions the spiritual sacrifices of the Christian. The eucharistic prayers of the Book of Common Prayer reflect this idea from 1 Peter: "We celebrate this memorial of our redemption, O Father, in this sacrifice of praise and thanksgiving." (BCP p. 363). Wednesday's reading may have been part of the homily offered to the converts just after their baptism.

Slaves and servants must submit to their masters. Everyone must submit to the authority of government. The ill treatment received at the hands of government and master gives the Christian an opportunity to participate in the redeeming suffering of Christ. These post-baptismal admonitions must be read in the light of Christian history, not as commandments for Christians to follow today. The church does not advocate passive acceptance of enslavement and oppression, but the message of 1 Peter is still relevant. Where Christian people suffer for the sake of justice and the Gospel, they are participating in the suffering of Christ.

Friday's text contains the one biblical reference to Christ's descent to hell between his death and resurrection. Even those in hell have a chance to repent and turn to Christ. This concept is expressed in the Apostles' Creed: "He descended to the dead. On the third day he rose again." The only other reference to Christ reaching out to the dead for salvation is found in Acts 2:27, which in turn is a quotation from Psalm 16:10: "For thou dost not give me up to Sheol, or let thy godly one see the Pit." Friday's reading of 1 Peter 3:13—4:6 could be a creedal statement recited by the Christian community at the time of the Easter baptisms.

The Gospel readings:

Guidelines for the primitive church continue on Monday with Jesus' words about divorce. If Torah allowed divorce, Jesus insists, it was only because God knew that the people were so hard of heart that they could not live under the full implications of God's intentions. Not so for the Christian. God created male and female to live as one. What God has joined together must not be separated. The celibate life is held out as an alternative to marriage, a unique statement found only in Matthew and in Paul's writing. We read Mark's version of Jesus' thoughts about divorce back during the week of the Sunday closest to August 10. I would repeat the point I made then. The church's authority to interpret God's continuing revelation (Matt. 18:18) has led to a new understanding of divorce in our time.

Our reading in Matthew on Tuesday, Wednesday and Friday parallel Mark's Gospel. Refer to my remarks in connection with the Gospel of Mark for Wednesday and Thursday, week of the Sunday nearest to August 10.

Thursday's reading is the parable of the laborers in the vineyard. God loves everyone totally. There are no favorites.

We conclude our liturgical year together this week. We'll celebrate a new year on Sunday, with the First Sunday of Advent. Advent 1, year 2 is your starting point in the daily lectionary next week.